SUCCESSWITH

SMALL-SPACE
GARDENING

GRAHAM CLARKE

SUCCESSWITH

SMALL-SPACE

GARDENING

GRAHAM CLARKE

THE GUILD OF MASTER CRAFTSMAN
PUBLICATIONS

First published 2010 by
Guild of Master Craftsman Publications Ltd
166 High Street, Lewes, East Sussex BN7 1XU

Text © Graham Clarke, 2010
© Copyright in the Work, GMC Publications Ltd, 2010

ISBN: 978-1-86108-665-5

A catalogue record of this book is available from
the British Library.

Associate Publisher: Jonathan Bailey
Production Manager: Jim Bulley
Managing Editor: Gerrie Purcell
Senior Project Editor: Virginia Brehaut
Editor: Judith Chamberlain-Webber
Managing Art Editor: Gilda Pacitti
Design: Studio Ink

Colour origination: GMC Reprographics
Printed and bound: in Thailand by KNP

Previous page: Good design
This small space has been carefully designed and crafted to include
a pathway, raised bed, containers, climbing plants and even a mirror
as an optical device.

Top: Perennial pleasures
A grouped planting of perennial hostas and lupins.

Middle: A contemporary look
Modern and contemporary gardens like this appeal to many people.

Bottom: Old-style herbs
This herb garden may be traditional in design, but it still does not
take up a lot of space.

→ CONTENTS

INTRODUCTION

For a host of reasons, gardens these days are getting smaller. In past times, those who were well off had the luxury of large gardens, with rolling lawns, a windbreak of tall trees or hedges, long herbaceous borders and large 'island' beds around which you could stroll. There were often sizeable kitchen gardens, fruit cages, a rose garden, a woodland walk, a large Victorian greenhouse (or even an orangery), ponds (or lakes) and, of course, a paved terrace that looked over the lawns.

Today, a few fortunate people are still able to enjoy these spacious trappings. The rest of us, however, must cram! The lack of outdoor space causes real consternation with keen gardeners. If there is room for growing vegetables they will nearly always be on full view; a single tree (if there is room for one) is likely to cast sufficient shade over the lawn (if there is room for one) so that it is permanently mossy and in poor spirits. Single roses can be accommodated, but the thought of a 'garden' or even a 'bed' devoted to them alone would be considered extravagant in the extreme.

I have always said that there is a far greater challenge in getting a tiny garden, balcony or courtyard looking good, than there is in creating a large garden that has oodles of room. The small-space gardener must be imaginative, innovative and hugely creative, whereas the large-space gardener can simply place a few large plants strategically and visitors will coo and congratulate him/her on a well-conceived planting scheme.

If all you have is a shady courtyard or a windy balcony or a sun-baked patio, then you will need to plan the space, consider the plants and juxtapose with plenty of thought. You will need to choose, plant and prune carefully. And if you get all of this just about right, your small garden will be every bit as breathtakingly beautiful as any large plot. In fact, it could be even better.

This book, therefore, is aimed at keen gardeners who are looking after a small area. The space itself may be newly acquired, or the gardener may have just taken an interest in making the area look nice. It will also be of use to the person who has just bought a second home – something that is traditionally smaller than the main home and therefore with a smaller garden. It will still need to look good, but it will also need to be low maintenance as there could be long periods of time with nobody in residence.

We also hope that owners of balconies, porches, courtyards, patios, decks and front gardens will be able to glean information of value to them. With this book we are even aiming for the large garden owner who may be wondering what to do with a little corner or area.

In all these cases, this book will enthrall and encourage, and at the same time give you hard facts on what should and should not be done. Don't let a small garden put you off gardening!

Award of Garden Merit

Throughout this book you will see the initials AGM set after certain plants. This denotes that the plant in question has passed certain assessments carried out by experts under the auspices of the Royal Horticultural Society in Great Britain. Only plants with exceptionally good garden qualities can be awarded this special Award of Garden Merit.

→ **Make use of your small space**
Lighting, screening, furniture and plants make the use of this small-space garden functional and decorative.

01.

WHERE HAVE OUR GARDENS GONE?

Stylish small space

Detail and interest have been achieved in this very small
space with a simple water feature and informal planting.

MORE PEOPLE, LESS SPACE

With each day that passes, the earth is getting more heavily populated. More and more people are congregating in cities and towns, and their peripheries, which means that there is less personal space for individuals and a greater sense of congestion.

Land for building on is also becoming scarce, at least throughout the UK, in the more heavily populated parts of the US and throughout the richer European states. The land is gobbled up by construction work of all sorts, from roads and other transport networks, to industrial, office and retail complexes. Housing – much of which should have garden land attached to it – is just a small proportion of the increasing use of land. And don't forget, if arable and livestock areas are used for development, there is a very good argument to move them to reclaimed common or woodland, in order to maintain the food supply.

↓ Inner-city Paris

Although this is a view of an inner-city situation, it serves to illustrate the congested nature of our lives. Apart from the municipal area behind the domed building, there is hardly a space for home-grown greenery anywhere within the picture.

PACKING THEM IN

In this small space, the gardener has
been able to cram in so much in terms
of structure, planting, functionality and
ornamentation. Interest is provided in the
form of raised beds, which add height to
an otherwise flat area.

THE CONSEQUENCES OF LESS SPACE

This is a gardening book so we cannot really devote space to examining the sociological – and psychological – issues affecting large numbers of people in close proximity, but with regard to the particular theme of the book, it is an obvious fact that with more and more people vying for the same or adjacent pockets of land, there will be plenty of frustration, and in increasing intensity. In horticultural terms, this can be most profound.

The lack of space means people are housed in blocks of high-rise apartments and streets of close-set terrace housing with little or no land attached for gardening. The maximum number of dwellings must, it seems, fit into the minimum amount of space and that means the average sizes of gardens is diminishing, often in alarming proportions. For example, the gardens that are attached to newly built properties can be as little as 322 sq ft (6 x 5m), and this is certainly not the smallest that may be found.

And if spaces *have* been made available for gardens, they are likely to be in the form of small courtyards, porches or balconies. However, there is still plenty you can do with a small space whether it is growing plants in a window box, training plants over a wall or being imaginative with a pathway.

COURTYARDS

Originally a courtyard garden was a square or rectangular open space entirely surrounded by buildings, and modern developments are frequently constructed on this principle. These days the space could be a patio or hard-paved area with your home on one side and fences or walls of different purposes on the other three sides.

A typical courtyard will always have a regular shape and probably a central feature (such as a fountain, sitting area or just a sundial or piece of statuary). The best courtyards will always be symmetrical in their overall design and planting.

PATHWAYS

It is common to find pathways and alleys between rows of houses and between apartment blocks. So that they use up the minimum space, they are generally narrow and heavily shaded. Some passageways act like wind tunnels, which makes them unsuitable for growing most plants, even if there is space. The good news is that there are some plants suitable for these areas.

The passageway may have a concrete, paved or tarmac base, which means that plants cannot be easily planted into the ground without major demolition of the base. Growing plants in containers is a sensible option. However, don't forget that the walkway was designed for access, possibly even bulky loads, and it is all too easy to obstruct it with pots, tubs and hanging baskets.

↓ Shady courtyard

Traditionally, courtyards were surrounded on all sides by buildings. They could be suntraps, or heavily shaded, depending on the aspect and the heights of the buildings. Here a central tree dominates the space, causing much shade underneath.

↘ Make passageways interesting

This ugly area, a space separating two buildings, could be decorated with plants. It is big enough for containers not to cause an obstruction. And the open gate can be blocked in to provide privacy and some protection from wind.

VERTICAL GARDENING

Small-space gardening means that you should make use of the surfaces that are usually forgotten or ignored by gardeners with larger areas of land to play with, and here I am talking of the vertical surfaces – walls, fences, arches, pergolas and so on.

Walls and fences, particularly, are useful for supporting wall pots and hanging baskets. Even if there is just a few inches of soil at the base of a wall you should be able to grow a clinging climber, such as clematis, Virginia creeper, ivy and so on.

It may be feasible to create a greater planting area by lifting paving slabs or breaking up a concrete base perhaps. This will enable a greater selection of climbers to be grown and even one or two tender plants that require to be grown under the shelter of a wall rather than out in an open garden. And many of these climbers and wall plants can offer other benefits on top of being decorative; think of grapevines, passion flowers, hops, kiwi fruits and so on.

SMALL-SPACE TIP

If you have a passageway that is particularly windy, you will find a solid gate placed at one or both ends of the passageway will reduce the impact of the wind by a huge degree. However, check first that the land is yours and there are no covenants to prevent you from putting up gates in such places.

↑ **The golden hop**
Humulus lupulus 'Aureus' is a decorative climbing plant and, if you are keen on beer-making, it is productive, too.

← **Clothing walls with plants**
If space is tight on the ground, garden upwards. Climbers, wall plants and hanging baskets are used here to soften the hard lines of a yellow-bricked building.

CONTAINERS

If you live in a high-rise dwelling, with no ground space, you may be able to use window boxes, hanging baskets and wall pots to improve your outlook. Even if all you have is a patio, porch, a set of steps or a basement area, there are still many types of suitable containers and plants to go in them. These are discussed in full in Chapter 08.

↘ **Plantless balconies**
Here are a number of balconies on a high-rise apartment block and there is not one plant to be seen. Just imagine how much nicer – and greener – the building would look with foliage and flowers spilling out of troughs and baskets.

↓ **Variegated hosta**
Containers can be simple and subdued as in the case of this single pot with a variegated hosta or they can be complex and colourful. Whichever you choose, they can be moved and replanted to keep your small garden looking colourful and fresh throughout the year.

BALCONIES AND ROOF GARDENS

Some balconies are constructed to allow access to the exterior of a building for the purposes of maintenance. These are usually small and narrow with just enough room to stand on. Other balconies are designed to provide an outdoor space and may have room for some furniture and, of course, a few plant containers.

Some lucky inhabitants of apartment blocks may have access to a roof garden. There may be a decent amount of space, enabling you to be quite creative with the things you do. However, there will certainly be restrictions on what can and cannot be planted or created on the roof garden and you should ascertain fully who owns it before you do anything.

There will also always be one overriding problem that you will need to overcome – that of the wind. No matter how high the roof garden is, it will always seem to be a windy and exposed place. Fortunately there are wind-tolerant plants available and there are ways to minimize the impact of the wind, so you should not be deterred from making the most of the space if it becomes available to you.

So is it worth bothering with a garden when all you have is a small amount of space? The answer is indefatigably, yes. Just see what can be achieved, in terms of colour and pleasure, in a space just a few feet across. Even if you don't like gardening, a small space will be easier (and cheaper) to stock, plant and maintain.

JUST WHAT IS A SMALL GARDEN?

It's a difficult question to answer, for what is 'small' to one could be 'massive' to another. The definition really depends on your expectations and experience. For example, a beginner to gardening, or one who has lived in small accommodation for most or all of their lives may find that a plot measuring some 1,076 sq ft (10 x 10m) is quite big; it would more than likely provide enough of a challenge for their limited knowledge and resources, and therefore expectations.

Meanwhile, a more experienced gardener might not be satisfied with anything less than five times this amount, and may actually require something approaching half an acre (0.2ha).

WHY IS GARDENING SO IMPORTANT?

So, in conclusion to the question of where have our gardens gone, we should perhaps be asking the question: 'Why is it so important anyway?'

I am a gardener through and through, so I will argue vehemently for gardens to be made available to as many people that want them as possible, particularly as the more congested our lives become, the greater is our desire – and the need – for our own spaces.

In a garden we can open our lungs and breathe in the oxygen. And in some small way we can connect with Nature, even if it is just a tiny space and for a short time. Gardening fulfils a basic, instinctive need in all of us and it can relieve stress by providing a calm, refreshing oasis in our busy lives.

02

DESIGN BASICS FOR THE SMALL-SPACE GARDEN

Plants suggest style

With a small space at your disposal you can – with relative ease – choose the garden style of your dreams. Here, lupins and poppies occupying a small area give the impression of a cottage garden in all its glory.

START PLANNING

Given that you have a small area in which you wish to create a garden, how do you go about working out where to put certain plants or features? It is all in the planning. Every bit of available space must be considered, whether or not you decide to do anything with it. The important point is not to ignore anything, otherwise you may find yourself in the position of having completed the creation of your small-space garden only to realize that there is a gaping hole in a flowerbed, or that there is an expanse of brick wall or wooden fencing with no plants covering it.

↓ Perfect planning

There are many advantages to putting a plan on paper, not least that you can see the whole area from above and you do not have to use your imagination to see the changes. Graph paper is essential if you want to be accurate.

PUT THE PLAN ON PAPER

With the best will in the world it is impossible to provide a design here and now that will fit exactly into your plot and meet all your requirements. It is possible, however, for certain sections and features discussed in this book to be usefully applied to your garden, via a plan.

This needs to be a plan on paper, not just in your head. Designing on paper means the most uncompromising plot may become revealed as the garden of your dreams! The paper plan does not have to be perfectly created using special equipment – it can be decidedly more 'rough and ready' than that.

One of the main advantages of a paper plan is that different shapes of beds can be drawn and easily changed, and paths, patios, containers and so on can be put in position and then changed at will.

Also, the whole of your garden can be seen from above, which will give you the best idea of dimensions and proportions. And lastly, I always follow the maxim that if a plan looks right on paper, it will look right on the ground.

WALK THE AREA

It is generally best to start your survey of the garden space by walking around the house (and any outbuildings). Take a large note pad with you so that you can quickly draw the straight lines or 'edges' of the plot and the general layout – in plan form but not to scale.

The drawing must be large enough to include the measurement of all downstairs windows, doors, steps and so on. Include also any air vents in the walls and the position of existing climbing plants (if you wish to keep them).

↙ The professional touch
Professional designers often transcribe a design on to tracing paper so that it can be used as an overlay. Home designers do not normally need to go to these lengths.

↓ Taking a walk
It is important to walk around the garden, with paper and clipboard in hand, and draw the key plants and features that you wish to retain.

MEASURE THE AREA

In order to be relatively accurate in your plan, you will need to measure the space. It is worth spending a bit of time on this because you will end up with a plan that is to scale and resembles (in outline) the garden, making it much easier for you to visualize.

Ideally, you need a tape measure at least half as big again as the widest part of your garden; it needs to be this sort of length so that you can go around corners with the tape if required. You will also need a helper to hold the other end of the tape or, failing this, a metal spike to secure the end.

Start at one corner of the house and then lay the tape on the ground all down one side of the house. If there are bay windows or other protruding features it becomes a case of laying the tape as close to the house as possible and keeping it reasonably straight.

The use of boning rods

If the area is quite large or is on an incline, you may find some wooden pegs, a straight-edged board and a spirit level will help you establish levels. For even larger areas, boning rods may be required. These are T-shaped rods some 4ft (1.2m) long and with a cross-member 18in (45cm) long, set at right angles at the top. Get a helper to hold one in place (preferably with the base of the rod set on top of a peg that has been pre-set into the ground at a given height), and then you do the same with your rod. Check that the tops of the horizontal bars are in line. By doing this you can determine a new gradient, or make an incline level, although this is more usually the realm of professional designers and landscapers.

⏶ It takes two ...

One person can easily measure small areas, such as this pathway entrance. For longer distances, two people are better unless you can manage to anchor the end of the measuring tape whilst holding the reel.

SMALL-SPACE TIP

Be careful with angles when you are measuring, for it is quite unusual for a plot to be exactly square or rectangular, and the position of the house is not always exactly parallel to the boundaries.

THE DESIGN FRAMEWORK

The framework for the design will be set within the boundary lines of the garden and features such as the position of pathways and areas for seating. These will be determined by factors such as the position of the sun at certain times of the day or where there may be a good viewpoint.

Take into account also any immoveable objects such as manhole covers, telegraph poles and oil tanks. You may also have objects that at first glance appear immoveable, but which can in fact be repositioned such as ponds, greenhouses, sheds, driveways and so on.

And finally where the framework is concerned, whether a garden is big or small it is important to get the 'shape' right when designing and choosing plants. In a small plot this rule is particularly crucial, as errors will be viewed at close quarters and therefore appear disproportionately large. For example, if a taller tree is placed in front of a smaller shrub from the main viewpoint in the garden, then this will look wrong and will require effort and time to alter. It's much easier to get it right first time.

THE FRAMEWORK

When creating a plan on paper, start by considering the design framework: this includes the position of the boundary, paths, raised beds and the space for furniture (if required).

GOOD SPACING

Shrubs and trees must be given enough space to grow otherwise the other plants will become overcrowded and shapeless. In a small-space garden there is a definite temptation to buy too many plants, especially when they are small, and to plant them with little thought as to what their eventual size will be.

With advance planning, that is drawing the planting plan (at least for the main plant subjects) on paper and to scale, you can plant in such a way that you allow enough space for development. A good nursery catalogue will always give the height, spread and flowering time for perennials, bulbs, trees, shrubs, climbing plants and conifers. A good example of spacing is shown in the box above right.

⇘ Space to grow

When planting shrubs and perennials it is important that enough space is given for their natural development. This may mean that the bed looks fairly empty straight after planting.

HOW TO SPACE PLANTS

1. You choose, say, a *Rhododendron* and you are told that its width at maturity is 10ft (3m). There should therefore be a clear radius space, taken from the centre of the plant at planting time, of 5ft (1.5m). This will allow for the *Rhododendron* to grow and develop, unhindered.

2. At the same time you decide that you want to plant next to it, say, a *Camellia* which has a guide maturity width of 8ft (2.5m). This should be set with 4ft (1.2m) of clear radius space, and therefore some 9ft (2.7m) from the trunk of the *Rhododendron*.

SMALL-SPACE TIP

At the time of planting it will appear as though there is masses of space in the bed and it will look empty. As a temporary measure, and for a year or two until the shrubs concerned become sizeable, you can fill the spaces with annuals, bedding plants, bulbs, short-lived perennials or even position plants in containers.

↑ Odd numbers

It is almost always more pleasing on the eye for groups of plants to be grown together rather than individual specimens. Here three green hostas are sited next to seven lupins of different colours, and groups of other perennial and bedding plants.

GROUPING PLANTS

Some smaller shrubs and perennials make a much better feature if several of the same are planted close together in order to make one bold unit. Strangely, odd numbers of plants look better than even numbers, partly because plants do not grow in an even, orderly or symmetrical way (see box). For a group of objects to look 'right', the eye must be allowed to 'rest', and not be made to 'wander'. But there are limits: seven miniature roses planted in a bed may look better than six, but much more than that and the effect is lost.

THE RULE OF ODD NUMBERS

To understand the reasoning behind growing plants in groups of odd numbers, place four dots on a piece of paper so that they represent a square. Your eye will dart from one to another. Now, place one dot right in the middle of the other four and your eye will come to rest on the odd (fifth) dot. This is because the eye is happier with an odd number, or a central focal point, and it works well with small numbers of objects.

REFINING THE PAPER PLAN

If your intended small-space garden needs lots of hard landscaping (paving, walling, arches, pergolas, steps and so on), then the more accurate and precise your paper plan is, the better. For this reason it may be best to redraw the plan on to scaled graph paper. If you simply wish to change some of the planting with perhaps a new rustic pathway and some containers, then precision drawing will not be necessary.

The scale is the important next step. The most appropriate scales for garden work of this nature are approx. ½in = 1ft (1cm = 1m), or ¼in = 1ft (1cm = 0.5m). The first scale will produce a drawing twice the width and length of the first, so if the garden is large you may need a large sheet of paper. On the other hand, this larger scale does make it easy to name individual plants on a planting plan, and in quite small detail as well.

TRANSLATING FROM THE PLAN

When you are ready to get outside and translate what has been drawn on the paper plan into the three-dimensional garden, you may suddenly be daunted by what you are faced with. Do not panic. The important thing now is to be systematic. Whether you are changing an existing garden or starting with a bare plot, the order of work should be based on a definite schedule (see box below).

If you intend to conduct delicate operations, such as laying a lawn, then the use of heavy or bulky machinery should be carried out prior to starting the lawn. It is best to construct paths and paved areas at an early stage to improve access and, when it comes to making the lawn, this can be raised slightly above the paving, which helps when mowing.

↘ Hard landscaping

If your new garden is to include lots of hard landscaping (paving, walling and so on), then it is important for your paper plan to be as accurate as possible, otherwise you may be buying too many or too few materials.

WORK SCHEDULE

1. Clear the site – of plants, rubble, unwanted structures, etc.

2. Level the site – either to make it flat, or to create changes in level such as with raised beds or terracing, or even to create an incline where there is not one currently.

3. Add in drainage – incorporating an imperceptible gradient for water run-off, as well as soakaways or gullies leading into an existing drain.

TURNING YOUR PLANS INTO REALITY

1. This new home has a small piece of land just 15 x 25ft (4.5 x 7.6m). The builders, in this instance, left it as bare soil, but sometimes they will put it down to grass.

2. Here is the opposite view, looking down the garden, away from the house. Interim stepping stones have been laid from the house to the gate at the bottom.

3. Having decided on what they want, the owners have removed the rubble, then followed this by levelling and raking the area. Now they are using pegs to mark the position of the lawn.

4. Six months later, with the use of some quick-growing annuals, climbers and bedding plants, the garden has been created. The lawn has established nicely and the owners are delighted with their small garden.

03

SMALL COURTYARDS AND ENCLOSED PATIOS

Maximizing use

Courtyards can be functional as well as decorative.
Here there is seating, heating and screening – all aimed
to encourage the owner to make use of the courtyard.

CREATING A COURTYARD

In the centre of a town, space can be at a real premium. And not only can the lack of suitable space be a problem, but also that of light, for tall buildings surrounding a plot can cast most unwelcome shade. This means that sun-loving plants will be unable to grow in an optimum way.

Fortunately you can turn even a dingy backyard into a bright, oasis-like courtyard garden, with interesting flooring stones and bright walls that reflect the light. Add some lush green foliage, some plants in vases or urns, an 'architectural' tree or large shrub and perhaps even the sound of some running water, and the area will be completely transformed. Of course, it is never as easy as that!

⊾ Courtyard flooring

Design your courtyard so that it is both functional and decorative – here there is a pathway leading to an access point and there is shelter and plenty of attractive planting.

GENERAL COURTYARD DESIGN

If your courtyard is literally a space surrounded on four sides with walls and there is only one way into and out of it – through the back door of the house, for example – then the courtyard will be private, secluded and peaceful. This kind of space lends itself to a central feature of a water fountain perhaps or a sundial or statue. There could be flowerbeds and borders, possibly raised ones, all round the perimeter of the courtyard.

You may, however, have a courtyard that is awkwardly shaped, is open on one or more sides, is close to a main road, is overlooked by neighbours or perhaps it has walls of different heights. It could, of course, have all of these things. In this case the courtyard will more than likely have a lot of movement going on, with people requiring access. This means that the general design, and the floor surface, has to be planned with this movement in mind.

Each courtyard has its own ambience and it is up to you to decide what you would like. You may want to create a sense of peace and harmony with a traditional design or you could go for something more challenging and unpredictable with elements of surprise and excitement.

Modern and contemporary courtyards can utilize brightly coloured screens, mirrors, stainless steel, and a number of different and novel structures. This may be your preference, but be careful, as this kind of theme may not be in keeping with the style of building or surrounding walls.

← **Gravel flooring**

It is important to get the base or the flooring of the courtyard right; it should be practical, but also sympathetic to the surroundings. Here there is a gravel base in a sunny courtyard.

SMALL-SPACE TIP

To help you plan your courtyard, think about your house. Inside there are treasured possessions and the décor is both attractive and interesting to you. The home is a living space to be enjoyed, not a museum to be looked at. In the courtyard and on the patio, the same rules apply. The proportions need to look right, the planting and the people should gel and the materials used should marry together.

THE COURTYARD FLOOR

Unlike larger gardens, courtyards are rarely suitable – or large enough – to accommodate an area of lawn. To start with, courtyards are always going to have a predominance of shade. Even if they face in the direction of the most sun, the boundary walls are invariably high enough to cast shade on three sides for most of the day, and with a small courtyard this could mean that most of the ground is dark, which will be unsuitable for growing grass.

Paving is the main alternative to grass, but this can be an expensive option. Shingle or gravel may be a cheaper option, but a whole courtyard of this could look dull. Shingle – particularly the smaller grades – will find its way into the house and, in autumn, it can be very difficult to sweep clean of fallen leaves. Moss can also be a problem in heavily shaded areas, and this is difficult to eradicate on loose materials such as shingle.

ACCESS

Whatever the shape and size of your courtyard, the first thing to bear in mind is always that you ensure free access to and from all the doors and gates. You can always put down flowerbeds, ponds or other features just a short distance from the entrances, but you may need to accommodate the need for access by putting down a walkway or small bridge over the feature.

↗ Trelliswork

A courtyard does not always need to have solid walls. Here a secluded area has been created with wooden trelliswork panels. These will remain open to the elements until the climbing plants have fully clothed them.

← Making the access attractive

Access to and from a courtyard is important, but it need not be boring. By choosing an old wooden door, for example, a feature can be created.

PLANTING

This is the most important means of creating an atmosphere or 'feel' to a courtyard area. A courtyard or patio without plants looks bare, unloved and unfinished, so you should always allow space for the positioning of containers, beds or borders, perhaps shrubs and maybe miniature gardens in troughs. If children are not a permanent feature of the household, you could try growing plants in between the paving slabs.

If the courtyard is mainly used as a type of 'outdoor room' during the summer, then it makes more sense to concentrate floral displays for them. Traditional subjects are geraniums, petunias, antirrhinums and lobelia, and between these four plant types alone, near enough every flower colour (except black) is available. There are, of course, certain plants that flower and reach their decorative peaks for every season. Refer to the directory section (starting on page 120) to determine what's best for your situation.

Wherever possible the vertical surfaces should have planting spaces against them. There will always be a wall or fence somewhere that could be covered by a climbing plant. This could, indeed, transform the courtyard from one that looks bare, with plain horizontal and vertical lines created by the 'hard landscaping', into something that is horticulturally delightful with charm and individuality.

↗ **Raised beds**
Raised beds give a new dimension to the courtyard garden.

↗ **Planting and decking**
Planting here overspills onto the adjacent base, in this case wooden decking.

Beds and borders

An extensive raised border should provide enough space for a reasonable selection of shrubby and ground-cover plants as well as for climbers on fences and walls. These can be constructed from a number of materials depending, to some extent, on the surrounding walls and surfaces. Brick and stone are obvious possibilities. The main trouble with natural stone in a courtyard is that the stone could eventually become slippery and dangerous in areas of deep shade.

A good alternative to stone in this situation is strong timber walling – such as that afforded by railway sleepers. Timber could well fit in with your courtyard if you also have wooden fences or timber decking.

Sitting areas

Areas in which to relax, preferably in a sunny spot, are important in every garden, and just because a courtyard may not have the luxury of space, it does not mean that at the designing stage you should ignore the subject of relaxation.

If space is particularly tight and there is no room for a range of freestanding patio-style garden furniture, consider building seating into low walls. A low brick wall can be turned into a seat if it is given a moveable, slatted wooden seat and back. If you have room for freestanding furniture, the style you choose plays a major factor in establishing the atmosphere of your courtyard or patio. Ornate cast metal tables and chairs or traditional upright heavy teak items tell a different story to a few loungers dotted around.

When assessing the sort of furniture you need, ask yourself a series of questions to make sure you choose wisely (see box below).

↑ Choosing a good spot
You must choose carefully where to site garden furniture, but the best place is usually in the sunniest spot.

→ Garden furniture
These modern wrought iron table and chairs have just about enough room, sited as they are on a small, raised wooden patio.

SELECTING GARDEN FURNITURE

1. How much space do you have?
In fact, do you have room for furniture at all? Could walls serve as perching places? Your courtyard may already be bursting with containers, features, raised beds and overflowing plants: after your furniture is installed will there still be room to walk around?

2. How many items do you need?
How many people are in the family? How many will want to be in the courtyard at a given time? Are there children? Do you do lots of entertaining?

3. Should the furniture be light and portable?
Do you want to move items to other parts of the courtyard or patio, for example, to stay in the sun? If so, this is done more easily with lighter-weight plastic furniture rather than heavy wood or metal.

4. Where should you place the furniture?
The sunniest spot is best, but an alternative would be a place close to a water feature, or near to scented plants or perhaps even a vantage point with a view.

5. What about winter storage?
Some items – plastic and metal particularly – can generally stay in position all year round. Although this will hasten the degradation and staining of plastic furniture it should not make too much of a difference to metal furniture, provided it has had anti-rust treatment. Wooden furniture, however, really is better under cover in the winter. You may be able to buy a cover to slip over it whilst still in situ otherwise it is best moved to a shed or some other dry, undercover place.

WATER FEATURES

A water feature can often be particularly effective in a courtyard. Even a small pool has a beneficial effect out of all proportion to its size. For a pond, try not to have a surface area of water less than 6 x 6ft (2 x 2m) – maintaining a pool in good health is difficult if it is very tiny. The temperature of water, and its chemical content, can vary dramatically in short periods of time, and this causes difficulties for both animals and plants. It may also stimulate the formation of algae, blanket weed and other undesirables.

↘ Small water features

A water feature, even one with constant running water, need not take up much space.

Siting

Correctly siting a pond or other water feature is crucial. It is not advisable to build it adjoining or abutting the house wall, as you need access to the footings and damp course at all times. It should also be placed where it gets direct sunlight for at least part of the day, but it should not, if possible, be sited directly under a tree whether evergreen or deciduous. This is because it is not so much the falling leaves that cause a problem in the pond water, but other things that drop off the tree such as twigs, bark, insects, dust, bird droppings and so on.

Styling

In a courtyard, the water feature can be kept informal in outline, although a squared-off courtyard tends to demand formally shaped and constructed pools. Oblong, rather than square, seems to look better, but a circular one could be equally effective.

You may decide to purchase a plastic pre-formed pool, or instead opt to make one using heavy-duty butyl sheets as the liner. Today these are easier and more cost-effective than putting in a concrete-lined pool, which is excellent if correctly built, but if not is likely to be a worry with leaks and cracks in time or after extreme hot or cold weather.

WALL FOUNTAINS

If you cannot clothe the walls of your courtyard with plants, one option to add interest may be to create a wall fountain such as this 'green man' head. This will of course require a degree of skill and dexterity in terms of 'plumbing' with pump and piping behind the wall. You will also need adequate access. It may therefore be a good idea to ask an experienced landscaper to help you.

Supporting

With a rigid plastic pool, it is essential to make sure that the support it gets from the surrounding soil is even, all the way around. When the pool is filled with water it will be extremely heavy and stresses and strains on this kind of structure must be avoided. So when excavating the hole into which the rigid liner will be set, make sure it is deep enough to also accommodate a 2–4in (5–10cm) layer of sand before the liner goes in. And then pack the air gaps between the sides of the liner and the surrounding ground with sand or, of course, the spoil from the excavation. Make sure that there are no remaining air pockets prior to filling the inside with water.

INSTALLING WATER FEATURES

Having decided that your small-space garden would be improved by the addition of a specific type of water feature, you must then decide on when and how to install it. In terms of 'when', it is generally better to do this between late autumn and early spring – a period of the year when plants are not in active growth, so they can be transplanted or cut back effectively in order to accommodate your water feature with little or no lasting damage being done to them.

Also, choose a day when there is no wind, and the ground is neither frozen nor waterlogged. This will make the installation process, with any soil excavation, more comfortable – and practical.

In terms of 'how', this will depend on the type of feature you are installing. On these pages we are showing step-by-step sequences of putting in two different types of ground fountain.

INSTALLING A PEBBLE FOUNTAIN

The pebble fountain is a relatively modern concept which provides water movement and sound, but is generally safe for children and pets. Being a small, self-contained water feature, it is also perfect for garden or courtyards with restricted space.

1. With a spade, make a hole in which to fit the reservoir.

2. Line the hole with sand and place the reservoir into position, ensuring it is level.

3. Place the pump housing and nozzle and fill with water.

4. Arrange washed pebbles over the pump housing platform.

5. Surround the area with plants and paving – and switch on!

INSTALLING AN EGG-STYLE FOUNTAIN

1. Excavations are started for housing the fountain 'liner' or 'reservoir'. A layer of builders' sand is required in the base.

2. The liner is placed in to the hole to check for depth and level – a spirit level is crucial.

3. More sand is required to protect the sides and lips of the liner, and all edge levels should be checked.

4. Rubber tubing, which is cut to fit, needs to be threaded through the egg fountain and then connected to the pump.

5. The egg is placed into position, and a final check for levels is made.

6. Pebbles are placed over the inspection cover to complete the effect, and new plants surround the whole structure.

7. Within just a few weeks, the area looks established.

If you would prefer to see a piece of modern 'art' – something that would be both a focal point and a talking point – this smooth, high-density concrete egg fountain has a timeless, contemporary feel. Dimensions of the egg stone are: height 19¾in (50cm); width 15in (38cm) and weight 176lb (80kg).

04

ROOF GARDENS AND BALCONIES

Roof garden tree

The owner of this roof garden has taken a chance by planting a mature tree. There will need to be a good depth of soil; the roots are probably growing in a large, anchored container. Prior to installation, approval would be required, from both the local authority or council and by a structural engineer.

GETTING STARTED

With land at an absolute premium in most towns and cities, the use of flat roof and balcony spaces to create gardens in the sky is becoming more and more attractive. There are three principal factors that need to be considered before building a garden on such a structure (see box below).

ACCESS

Balconies are invariably designed to be accessed via purpose-built, full-length doors that lead straight on to them. Roofs are different: there may be similar doors, but often there are smaller points of access, where you can clamber out. You may have a roof space that has the perfect aspect and is just the right size, but will you be able to carry equipment and plants up to it?

↘ Small corner balcony

Container plants, twiners and trailing plants are being used to decorate and enhance this small corner balcony.

FACTORS TO CONSIDER

1. You must check that the roof is strong enough for you to build a garden there in the first place.

2. A suitable type and amount of growing medium – whether it is soil, bagged loam or peat – must be selected for the purpose.

3. The design of the garden and choice of plants should take into account the greater extremes of weather often experienced at a higher level around buildings, particularly the effects of the wind.

SMALL-SPACE TIP

Keeping the weight of all materials used in creating a roof or balcony garden to a minimum is a good policy to adopt, not only to ensure that you keep the overall loading to an acceptable level, but also because all these materials will have to be transported up to the roof by some means, in many cases it will be by hand.

THE FLOOR

The floor of the roof or balcony garden should be waterproof, particularly if there is living space immediately below. And since there is likely to be considerably more run-off where regular watering is taking place than from the equivalent space on which there are no plants, you should check that the provision for drainage is adequate.

In a well-designed roof garden there will be an area for sitting, and to save weight arguably the best surfaces would be very thin paving-quality slate or lightweight timber decks, or a combination of both. Naturally weathered wooden decking consists of very thin battens of pressure-treated softwood, laid and fixed to shallow, similarly treated wooden bearers. The whole structure should be restrained and prevented from moving sideways. For this reason it should be fixed to permanent side walls where available.

Gravel and shingle are alternative surfaces. These tend not to be so comfortable to put furniture on as they are not level and will 'move' quite a bit. However, they are lighter weight than paving slabs. Shredded bark is another lightweight option though it can look messy after a while and tends to get scuffed about.

Artificial turf is another option that is used by many roof gardeners; when laid well it can look attractive and can certainly enhance the garden 'feel' of a roof garden in a city. It is also lightweight and cheaper than hard or stone surfaces. But it must be anchored with appropriate glues and sealants, and it will probably need replacing after a few years.

GRAVEL FLOORING

In this instance, gravel has been used for the floor of a roof garden. This is a lighter weight material than stone slabs, but it is not as suitable for garden furniture.

SMALL-SPACE TIP

If you are working with both decking and paving of some form, then it is a good idea to abut the two and to seal or cement the joins. Provided the decking structure is even and level, it does not need to be fixed directly to the roof. For slate pieces, use a waterproof adhesive rather than a more traditional sand-cement mortar, which would be much heavier.

ROOF GARDEN FEATURES

Screens

Swirling winds and eddies are commonly found around and over the tops of buildings, and in order to provide some shelter from these, it is a good idea to fix screens between posts set at the perimeter of the roof garden. These screens may be made of clear plastic or toughened glass, or an opaque material if privacy is sought.

For a keen gardener, of course, trellis panels are probably the best option. If they are arranged carefully you will ensure that, regardless of the wind direction, there will always be at least one relatively sheltered spot somewhere in the garden. Whatever is chosen, it must be erected properly and to local building regulation standards. For this reason it is worth consulting the appropriate department at your local authority.

Pergolas

These can be an attractive option on a roof garden, if there is space for them and there are no weighting issues. Pressure-treated timber, in natural or coloured tones, should be used for the pergolas (as well as posts for trellis panels and other screens). Wherever possible, these posts should be bolted either to the balustrade wall or the building itself to provide extra strength and rigidity and to take as much load as possible away from the centre of the roof.

Ornaments

Statues, figures, sundials, boulders and so on, can all be heavy, so as with the containers (see pages 44–45), it is generally best to go for lighter-weight plastic, fibreglass or moulded-resin options.

Wooden planters

Many roof garden owners choose these for both practical and aesthetic reasons; they certainly seem at home on a roof garden. If such wooden planters are sited against the balustrade or other building wall, heavy-duty polythene or builders' damp-proof membrane should be fixed to the inside of the back of the planter. This helps retain moisture in the compost (particularly useful in summer), but also prevents damp from staining the outer face of the wood – and, in severe cases, from escaping onto the exterior walls where mould and moss could grow.

PERGOLA COVERED IN WISTERIA

If your roof garden can support the weight of a pergola – make sure that the wooden uprights are situated over supporting walls – one of the finest plants to grow on it is Wisteria. Not only will it provide useful colour for several weeks in spring, but the scent of the flowers is delicious. Be careful, though, as it can be rampant.

Water and electricity

If the roof garden is large and strong enough, you could consider a small water feature. The sorts of ideas discussed in courtyard gardens (see previous chapter) will generally be quite at home on a roof garden, too. Remember that, if you wish to have moving water (as in a small fountain or cascade), then you will need to have a power supply. The whole subject of electrical safety must be treated with great caution. If there is no existing supply, you must get a qualified and certified electrician to make the installation for you. If there is an existing supply, before you do anything, get it checked out by a professional, who will make sure that it is fully waterproofed.

↗ Pot fountain
A small self-contained water feature, such as this pot fountain, will make a roof or balcony garden really come to life.

↗ Water towers
This slightly more sophisticated water feature is still light enough to be used on a roof – even better if the weight is spread out by being supported on wooden decking.

↗ Water and light
Your water feature can be made to look really stunning with the combined use of contemporary ornamentation and lighting set to illuminate certain features.

↗ Lighting
Lighting a roof garden or balcony can take many forms; these are simply outdoor spotlights that are neither expensive nor difficult to install.

USING CONTAINERS

Pots, tubs, urns and vases can be made from heavy concrete, reconstituted stone, solid wood, metal and terracotta. These are all very weighty options though. It would be better to choose lighter plastic, fibreglass or moulded-resin containers – which are infinitely lighter and available in a multitude of styles and colours, many of which are made to look like their heavier cousins anyway.

Once the lighter-weight container is chosen, it will still become heavy once it is filled with the growing media of your choice. Soil and loam are heavy, especially when they have become saturated from heavy rainfall. Composts without soil, such as peat, coir and other mixtures are much lighter, but they need more frequent watering and their lightness might require you to somehow anchor them down to stop them blowing over in high winds.

Wooden pallets help to spread the load of larger and heavier containers. In any case, it is a good idea to raise containers off the ground, both for good drainage and also to prevent root growth emerging unnoticed through the base of the pot and then damaging the roof surface.

Finally, make sure that containers can be moved fairly easily so that access to the floor and side walls, as well as the outside of the building generally, is still possible. Resist the temptation to balance pots on the edges of balustrade walls; sooner or later these will blow or fall off and are bound to be broken or even cause damage to property or people.

↗ Themed summer display
Containers are a 'must' for most roof gardens; here we have a simple trough planted with *Amaranthus*, *Iresine* and *Cuphea*.

↗ Effective single planting
Classic freestanding containers, such as this metal urn, may look better with just one plant type in it rather than a mixture of colours. Here we have *Verbena Tukana* Hot Pink & Salmon.

SMALL-SPACE TIP

If you are growing bedding plants, annuals or bulbs, one way to lighten the load of the container is to fill the bottom half, at planting time, with polystyrene chunks (the sort that is sold for packing). This is so light, yet bulky, that it can reduce the weight of a container by between a quarter and a half (depending on what types of plant one needs the container for). The polystyrene also will aid the container's drainage potential: this can be a boon in winter when soil never really dries out, but it can be a

problem in a hot summer, when water seems to evaporate within an instant. Some roof gardens (balconies to a lesser extent) allow for a reasonable depth of soil. It may be tempting, therefore, to construct raised soil beds rather than use containers, but I would urge caution on this. The extra weight, plus drainage problems and the risk of damage to the property through penetrating damp, make this a much less desirable option.

↗ Herbs and strawberry plants

Even a few simple pots can convert a bleak-looking balcony into something green and interesting: the fact that the plants are also used in the kitchen is a bonus.

↗ Splash of colour

Vibrant colours can be had from planting nasturtiums in a bed next to some wooden decking. Strategically placed ornamental stones can hide any ugly edges.

↗ Light-weight tiles

This border could easily be in a garden at ground level. The bed has a 7in (17.5cm) depth of soil, and some of the larger plants are in containers. The pathway is laid with light-weight – but frost-hardy – ceramic tiles.

↘

PLANT CHOICE

Plants should be selected to provide enough screening and shelter (particularly by the climbers) without becoming too dense and thereby cutting out light from the garden space and, indeed, the house. To achieve this, the climbers growing on trellis panels, for example, should be deciduous so that in the generally shorter, gloomier days of winter, the maximum amount of light and low sun can penetrate through the leafless stems.

Some suitable climbers are Golden hops (*Humulus lupulus* 'Aureus'), summer-flowering honeysuckles (*Lonicera* spp) and climbing roses (such as 'Danse du Feu' and 'Aloha') and are also fairly tolerant of the exposed nature of roof gardens.

If the roof or balcony will be used in winter as well, then it is a good idea to incorporate some low-level evergreen plants for their year-round leaf presence. Ivies are, in many ways, the perfect choice. There are masses of species and varieties available, many with highly attractive and variegated foliage; they are tough plants as well, tolerating wind, drought, wet soil, extremes of temperature, bright sun and dense shade, and, importantly where small gardens are concerned, they cling close to the walls and therefore take up hardly any space at all.

If the more vigorous or larger-leaved types of ivy are grown, they just require a light trim annually to maintain their appearance and to keep them within bounds. There is a danger that if they are allowed to get out of hand, they are inclined to swamp other plants and also to create shade which may be undesirable. But I would always include a few ivies in any of my planting schemes.

Within containers a good selection of lower growing plants should provide both foliage and flower interest. The plants should be tolerant of wind, periods of soil dryness and also the extremes of microclimate that are often found on roofs. Many of the ornamental grasses, such as the blue fescue, *Festuca glauca* 'Blaufuchs', are ideal for containers.

← **Ornamental grasses**
The blue fescue is just one of the many ornamental grasses that are suitable for balcony and roof gardens.

← Rose 'Aloha'
This deciduous climbing rose is also tolerant of the windy conditions found higher up on buildings – but it needs to be tied in well to supports, such as wires or trellis panels.

← Evening fragrance
Honeysuckles will provide masses of fragrance on a still, warm summer's evening.

WATERING PLANTS

With a roof garden the expense of installing a tap and water supply is probably a wise investment. With a balcony, it is usually simple enough to carry out water from the kitchen or bathroom. In either case, however, it is important not to waste water. Home water metering, plus the fact that the cost of having water supplied is continually rising, are both good reasons for conserving water at home. But how is it best applied on a roof or balcony?

← Soaker hoses
These hoses are permeable along their length and when the tap is turned on water seeps through the sides, which makes the ground become thoroughly moistened.

↗ Irrigation pipes
These pipes, permanently connected to a rooftop tap, can be laid around the area – just turn the tap on and all of the plants will get watered.

↗ Watering cans
For most balconies, and the smaller roof garden, a watering can may be all that is needed. They are available in metal or plastic, and come in a range of sizes.

Watering cans

This provides the most direct and efficient watering of any device. Can sizes vary, from a house plant up to a big 2 gallon (10 litre) can. The design you choose is simply a matter of personal preference and what feels comfortable. The old-style metal watering cans are coming back into fashion. They usually have relatively long spouts, which makes for easy pointing and direction of water flow.

Drip-irrigation systems

You can buy, at reasonable cost, a complete drip-irrigation system for the roof garden or balcony (or a section of it, for example, just the containers). Pipes and branches of pipes with pre-drilled holes along their length can be laid throughout the area to be watered. When they are connected to a tap and it is turned on, the water seeps out of the holes and soaks the immediate area.

SAFETY

The final word on roof and balcony gardens has to be 'safety'. You must ensure that the edge of the garden that is not enclosed by screens or trelliswork is made absolutely safe and secure. This is especially the case if the balustrade wall is lower than 3ft (90cm). You may need to install some form of horizontal guard rail, which could be made from materials sympathetic to the garden such as similar timber to that used in the other features.

If the roof or balcony garden is on a reasonably modern building, and access to it is through full-length doors, then it is fairly safe to assume that it has been constructed to a sufficiently high standard and can therefore be used as a private garden. A problem may arise with older buildings, however. Wear and tear may have weakened the structure, and in any case building standards were much lower in the past.

In all matters of safety and the regulations concerning building roofs and balconies, talking to your local authority or a qualified structural engineer should set you right.

↗ Small balcony
This balcony is so small that it has room just for a few potted plants. Yet with careful choice of plants (including the colourful paper plant, *Bougainvillea*), a decorative and worthwhile area can be created.

↘ Trailing plants
More *Bougainvillea* is seen here, along with many trailing plants, which give the balcony planting structure and interest.

SMALL-SPACE TIP

Take particular care if the space immediately beneath your roof or balcony garden does not belong to you, since you will be held responsible for any damage to the property caused by your activities. Third-party insurance cover should be arranged, and you should check that your garden is covered by your own house and contents insurance. If the property is rented, it is always a good policy to obtain the landlord's agreement to your gardening ideas first.

PATHWAYS, STEPS AND ENTRANCES

Path to success

Pathways may be constructed for purely ornamental reasons or, as in this case, for the functional purpose of taking someone from one part of the garden to another.

TYPES OF PATHS AND PATIOS

The structure of your pathway (and patio for that matter) should be designed and constructed to suit the purpose it is to serve. There is a wide range of materials available, to suit every possible gardening need, so you must shop around before deciding which you want.

Pathways that are essentially functional – in other words, they are needed to take people walking from one place to another – should be laid with practicality in mind, rather than for the aesthetic qualities. For example, providing there is sufficient space, don't skimp on the width of the pathway; it is frustrating for people if they have to walk around the garden in single file.

At the other end of the spectrum is what are called 'casual' pathways. These often lead nowhere particular and are usually created just for effect, such as stepping stones through a flowerbed. These paths can be much less formal in style and constructed lightly.

HARD PAVING MATERIALS

Pathways and patios need to be of a sturdy material and properly made. Ideally they should be in keeping with the character of the house and the general appearance of the garden. The same goes for steps and other changes in level. Patios tend to comprise multiple or single-colour paving slabs or brickwork.

Bricks and paviors
These can look very good in a rustic or cottage garden setting. They are ideal for pathways that have to be both functional and decorative.

Paving slabs and flagstones
These can appear quite boring, especially over a large area, so it is usually best to mix them with other materials. For example, strips of beach pebbles can be mortared into place between the slabs, or a narrow strip of shingle or gravel either side of a pathway can look very pleasing.

↗ **Paving and gravel**
Paving stones on their own can look boring. If they are integrated with other materials such as gravel, they are more interesting.

↗ **Laying brick paviors**
Brick paviors make a pleasing and durable surface. Modern-style paviors like these look best when used in a modern property.

↗ **Plants between paving slabs**
Plants growing in amongst paving slabs can effectively break up the hard lines of the landscaping material.

CRAZY PAVING

After the Second World War there was a considerable amount of broken masonry available and crazy paving was one of the results. It went through several decades of high popularity, though in recent years it has become less fashionable. However, it is still the first choice for many. But use it with caution.

1. When laying crazy paving, it is important to place the pieces first, so that you are happy with the general design, and specifically which piece fits well with the other pieces around it.

2. Because small pieces of paving can be unstable, always make sure that every piece is properly bedded on a good mortar mix.

3. Use a spirit level to make sure that every piece is level; make sure you test the level across several directions before you move on to the next piece.

4. Crazy paving can be most pleasing to the eye – and can usefully use broken paving that would have no other purpose. Be careful of using strongly coloured stone, however, as it is not to everyone's taste.

LOOSE PAVING MATERIALS

There is quite a lot to think about if you want to choose a looser paving material such as shingle, gravel, scalpings or bark products.

Shingle

Most shingle available is collected from river-bed deposits and as such it is usually made up of rounded stones. It is graded in size into pebbles 5mm, 10mm, 20mm and so on. The colours are mostly brown, yellow or cream/white. Shingle never seems to compact very well, which means that it always seems to be moveable. A depth of more than 1in (2.5cm) or so can be difficult to walk on, so the usual recommended depth is just three or so stones deep. The problem with this is that the stones are easily scuffed out of place, and so the base – whether it is soil, concrete, a fabric mulch or compacted hoggin (the best) – is exposed. Shingle does, however, give a very satisfying 'crunch' underfoot.

Gravel

Unlike shingle, this is usually made up from more angular stones, often as a result of crushing rock. However, like shingle, those which have been washed and graded tend to be reluctant to compact. Some gravels are made up from several stone sizes together with some dust and these do compact better to produce a reasonably stable surface. This could be used to a thickness of about 1in (2.5cm), although its use will still depend partly on the type of base. Gravels are available in a wide range of sizes and colours.

Scalpings

This is a mixture of relatively large and small pieces of crushed rock, mixed with rock dust.

⌐ Paving and coloured gravel
Gravel and shingle are popular surfaces and these days designers often like to use some of the wide range of colours available.

When compacted it can produce a very hard surface, but is not very attractive. The larger stones may kick out and it is really only used as a base for patios, paths and driveways. Its compacted thickness beneath a pathway taking foot traffic could be some 3–4in (7.5–10cm).

Bark products

There are a number of products derived from trees, which can be spread over the ground to produce an attractive surface. The bark from a number of different trees is available in various

↗ Bark 'chips'
Shredded and pulverized bark is a soft, safe and ultimately very good surface for walkways, especially in an informal or woodland setting.

↗ Woodland bark path
Bark paths tend not to be slippery when wet, making them safe for children. In fact, many playground surfaces are made from bark products.

grades, most usefully as 'chips'. These can be spread over planted borders as a mulch against weeds, or onto compacted ground as a pathway. In the latter case, a depth of 2–3in (5–7.5cm) is all that is required.

Brown – or natural – colouring is the most popular, but these days the bark is also available in stained colours from golds and greens, to vivid reds and black. All the products available have a texture that goes well in a woodland setting or in a wild garden.

SMALL-SPACE TIP

Bark products, being unstable, can sometimes be 'walked' into the home and, if they are wet, they will stain carpets. So it is a good idea to make sure that you only use them some way from house doors and not as a patio base adjoining the house.

EDGINGS

All shingle, gravel and bark pathways have to be contained by edgings or kerbs. Even brick or slab paths look smarter if they have a neat or interesting edging.

These edgings might be made from brick, natural stone, concrete, timber or plastic. Where shingle and gravel are concerned, it is best to have the surface at least 1in (2.5cm) below the rim of the edging. Bricks, set on their sides, on end, or set at an angle of about 45 degrees are commonly seen.

If you have an older-style property it would make sense to choose a Victorian or Edwardian style of edging, such as a wrought iron edging or an ornate terracotta edging.

PLANTS AND PAVING

Plants look attractive and soften the harsh outline of a flat pathway or patio area. They are easy to use with crazy paving or any path edged with gravel. It may be necessary to excavate small holes and fill them with a good potting mixture and then sow or plant into these prepared pockets of good soil.

Some of the best plants to use for areas likely to be trodden on regularly are chamomile, thyme (*Thymus serpyllum*) and *Cotula squalida*. For areas that are not likely to be trodden on a regular basis there are many more good candidates such as snow-in-summer (*Cerastium tomentosum*), bugle (*Ajuga reptans*) and thrift (*Armeria maritima*).

↗ **Brick edging**
An edging finishes off a pathway or patio area. In fact, it is usually considered essential if the path surface comprises materials such as shingle, gravel or brickwork.

↗ **Plants in paving**
Careful positioning of plants can help to soften the edges of hard landscaping, particularly if they are allowed to flow over stone rather than being trimmed back regularly.

GREEN WALKWAYS

Grass, as a type of garden floor, is not really a viable option in the small-space garden. Apart from the shade that is usually found in such spaces, which is detrimental to the growth of grass, the amount of maintenance that is required in looking after a lawn would be completely disproportionate to the area given over to it.

Then there is the simple practicality of things like cutting it; have you tried to use a lawnmower to cut a lawn just a few meagre feet across? It's not easy.

However, for those who do want a green, living floor in their small space garden, arguably the best option would be to plant a lawn of chamomile, which may be found under either of its accepted Latin names: *Anthemis nobilis* or *Chamaemelum nobile*.

Chamomile is a lush, pale green, creeping herb that releases a pleasant fragrance when crushed underfoot. It has small, rather feathery, aromatic leaves and white daisy flowers, though the non-flowering 'Treneague' is preferable as a lawn, as the flowers of the other forms tend to spoil the close-carpeted effect.

It is the classic grass substitute and has been grown in this way for centuries. It does grow, although at a much slower rate than grass, and often you can just use shears to clip back the straggly stems.

However, it is bruised easily, so does not endure heavy foot traffic; nor is it a practical proposition for a children's play area. It is also difficult to control weeds in a chamomile lawn; if you think about it the chamomile itself is a weed and therefore precludes the use of all selective weedkillers.

PLANTED PATH

This pathway has been created more with decoration and plant use in mind, rather than as a functional walkway. Although there are paving stones set at 'pace' intervals, this pathway is certainly not designed for heavy foot traffic.

SLOPES

Whatever the size of garden, if it is on a slope it is more difficult to 'design' than one on the level. There are practical problems: for a start, many garden features such as patios, ornaments, sheds, ponds, greenhouses and so on, all need a level base before they can be built or placed.

If a garden slopes towards the house, it is important to introduce a flat area, say for a patio. This will look most appealing, even if you look up to it from house level. It will enable you to use

containers and put down seating where before it would have been impossible. A raised patio is the practical solution also to a garden that slopes down and away from the house. It creates a vantage point; a terrace from which you can overlook the rest of the garden. On a flat site, simply raising the level by perhaps 6in (15cm) may be sufficient to give the patio another dimension.

There are three main ways in which a level area, or 'terrace', can be created in a sloping garden. It can either be 'cut out' with the soil put somewhere else, or it can be filled in using imported soil/rubble, etc., or it can be a mixture of both of these.

⬐ Heather alongside steps

Plain grey steps can look dull, unless they are enhanced by planting. Here there are low hedges of heather (*Erica* spp), clipped and moulded to follow the direction of the steps.

⬐ Planting between steps

Old brick steps here with sympathetic planting, including chives, bugle and sage.

STEPS

In most cases, there will need to be a walkway linking parts of the garden on different levels and here there are two options: a sloping path (which can be awkward and dangerous in wet or icy weather) or steps. Steps are certainly the favoured option for a steep slope.

Assuming the steps are wide enough, you could place pots of bright flowers on them to produce a ribbon of colour. However, make sure the steps are not obstructed in any way. If there is no space on the steps, use a group of containers filled with flowers at the top and/or bottom to draw the eye up or down.

If there are likely to be elderly or infirm people using the steps it would be wise to construct some form of hand rail alongside, following the line of the steps. This rail should be at hand-height, and be sturdily fixed into place.

⭘ Steps softened by plants
A small flight of steps is enhanced by a low retaining wall, with plantings of ferns and small campanulas.

⭘ Woodland steps
This sloped, woodland garden has a flight of steps. Although the steps are made out of concrete, for stability, they are fashioned to look like tree sections or logs.

ENTRANCES AND ARCHES

Entrances – and the pathways leading to and from them – are particularly important because they give visitors their first impressions of your garden and home. They also make excellent focal points in a garden and can add an atmosphere of mystery and promise from whichever side you are viewing them.

In most houses, you enter through a gateway and then along a pathway to the door, which will naturally form the focal point to which the eye is led. Therefore it is worth making it

attractive and, where possible, well planted to reinforce the whole ambience of the entrance. Archways, which are basically open gateways where one crosses from one area to another, even if it is within the same garden, work best if the areas on either side of the opening are laid out in contrasting style, or are visually very different to each other. In a long, narrow space, for example, you could produce a series of arches or gates, taking the eye further on into an enticing journey of exploration.

← Path and old doorway
An old brick wall borders this small cottage garden and inset is a doorway that is totally in keeping with the style. It is always important to keep the access to such doorways clear.

SMALL-SPACE TIP

If you have a short pathway you can make it look longer by planting large plants at the boundary, or at the 'road end', and then smaller plants as you get closer to the house. To give the doorway more emphasis, place larger plants next to it, with smaller plants immediately in front of them. This situation will often be formal, with symmetrical planting either side of the door and pathway. In fact, it may be a classic approach, but a pair of identical standard or trimmed plants, such as bay or box, either side of the door looks wonderful.

↗ Designer gate

Simple garden gates can be boring, so why not choose something contemporary or 'funky'?

↗ Plants around front door

This cottage has an old brick pathway leading to the well-maintained – and planted – front door.

↗ Gate and archway

A brick archway framing a black wrought iron gate is traditional and homely.

↗ Wrought iron artistry

A low or half-gate made from wrought iron and painted black makes a perfect entrance to a formal garden setting.

06

WALLS AND FENCES

Brightening up a brick wall
Plants, even if they are in freestanding pots,
prevent a wall from looking stark and uninteresting.

VERTICAL GARDENING

When you garden in a small space, to make effective use of what you are given, you should use the surfaces that are generally forgotten or ignored by gardeners with larger areas of land to play with – and here I am talking of walls and fences. Even the dankest and dingiest corners can be brightened up with some well-chosen plants – and a little imagination.

And, when you think about it, there is a huge difference between having only a vertical wall on which to grow a plant or two, and having even the tiniest horizontal space in which to set a plant close to the wall, or to site a few floor containers.

↗ Contrasting foliage
Part of this house wall is covered with the dense foliage of climbing *Hydrangea* and variegated *Euonymus*. The two different types of foliage have grown into each other and become a feature.

TYPES OF WALL

When we think of high walls (as opposed to low types, such as retaining walls), there are three main types. As well as your own house wall, there may be dividing walls and probably boundary walls. You can use all of these to support plants.

House or building walls

The wall of your own home – or that of your neighbour's home – is there primarily to provide insulation and protection against the weather and will be constructed to ensure you get that protection. Assuming the building has been built within the past 200 years or so there will be damp proof courses and cavities, which may be filled with insulation material.

Dividing walls

These are used to divide one part of the garden from another. Their presence generally indicates that the garden is large and therefore needs to be segmented or partitioned off. Often these will be low walls, say from 1–4ft (30–120cm). They serve the same purpose as a taller wall, of course, but in a small-space garden they are to a more appropriate scale.

Modest garden walls like these are much easier to build than tall ones, which may need substantial reinforcing piers.

Boundary walls

These are the demarcation between your property and that of your neighbour or public rights of way. As such they should be sturdily built and therefore you can be safe in the knowledge that they are unlikely to fall on top of anyone. You may also wish for them to be tall for reasons of privacy and security.

↗ **Screen block boundary wall**

Boundary walls, to separate your property from your neighbours' or from public rights of way, can take many forms. This one uses traditional screen-block walling.

↗ **Spring climber**

This climber, *Clematis montana* 'Rubens', in full flower during mid- to late spring, can completely clothe a wall or fence.

↗ **Dry-stone boundary wall**

The ancient craft of building dry-stone walls still thrives; however, it should really only be employed on a country or rustic property; it would look incongruous forming the boundary of a modern garden.

DIVIDING WALL

This garden wall, with an arched gateway, was put up as a divider to separate one part of the garden from another. In most situations where this type of garden device is employed, as you pass through the gate you usually enter an area of the garden with an entirely different feel, such as from a formal to an informal area, or the other way round.

TYPES OF FENCE

Choosing to erect a fence, rather than a wall, is often based on financial considerations. But many people choose a fence for aesthetic reasons, especially if they are looking for a particular style of fence. Fences come in a variety of styles and colours or you can repaint or stain them to give the effect you wish to achieve.

Timber

Timber panels, which are usually larch wood, include horizontal overlapping strips, interwoven strips and close boarding with vertical feather-edged boards. Pallisade fencing is the term that is given to close-boarded timber mounted on arris rails between posts. There is also 'hit and miss' fencing with gaps between the timber boards; posts and horizontal wood rails (sometimes referred to as 'ranch' fencing); chestnut fencing where vertical pieces of chestnut are held by two or three

↗ Horizontal strips fencing
A traditional look is to be had with this natural-coloured fence comprising horizontal wooden strips.

↗ Picket fencing
There is no mistaking picket fencing, invariably painted white and with shaped tops to the wooden boards. This style of fencing is most suited to cottage and ranch-style properties.

↗ Wooden panel fencing
Wooden fencing panels constitute the most popular type of garden fencing. The panels are available in small, medium and full heights and are usually around 6ft (2m) across.

horizontal twisted wires; and picket fences of short, intermittent vertical timbers, usually with rounded or pointed tops.

Wire and steel

Fences made from these materials are usually destined for utility areas such as schools and industrial premises. They include chain link, wire or chicken netting, or even strained horizontal – the least secure type. Vertical railings and wrought iron fences are made from steel.

'Natural' screens

Natural screens are those made from bamboo, woven willow, hazel, heather, reed and so on. They are available in panels but the bamboo screens can also come as rolls. As with fencing panels, these screen panels should be wired on to pre-set posts.

↗ **Coloured fencing**

This small-space garden has a wooden fence – but it is like no other. The owner has opted for open-boarding, with the timbers painted different colours. This is fully in keeping with the rest of the space, where other bright colours are employed.

↗ **Bamboo screens**

Ornate screens, such as the one shown here, look particularly good in an informal or even woodland garden.

SMALL-SPACE TIP

Always make certain that any wall or fence that is to support a climbing plant is in a good state of repair before planting against it. Loose, crumbling mortar or rendering, unstable bricks, tiles that can be dislodged, or rotten weatherboarding or fencing, will only be made worse by attaching plant supports or training self-clinging climbers against them. Carry out any necessary repair work before planting. Where a wall or fence does not belong to you, make sure you have the permission of its owner before attaching any fixings.

PLANTING AREAS

It may be feasible to create a useful planting area near to the wall or fence (by lifting paving slabs, or breaking up a concrete base, for example). If this is done, a greater selection of climbing plants can be grown and even one or two tender plants that need the shelter of a wall rather than being exposed in an open garden. A house wall is often a particularly good place to grow a scented climber, such as honeysuckle or jasmine.

Not all walls and buildings are things of beauty, of course, so sometimes plants can be used to disguise them. You can also extend the height of a wall or fence with trelliswork to act as a screen or provide you with extra privacy.

WALL CLIMBERS AND SUPPORTS

Although there are plenty of plants that can cope by themselves against a wall, plants such as ramblers, scramblers, climbers and loose, flexible shrubs must have support. It should be reliable, safe and preferably almost invisible. Failing this it should be neat, aesthetically pleasing and ideally need as little maintenance as possible.

There are two main methods of support: a form of trelliswork or a series of taut wires held close to the wall. A third, less satisfactory option, may be to hammer in masonry nails or staples wherever they are needed. Wires can be attached to these and tied to the stems of the plants. For advice on planting climbers, see page 110.

↗ **Adding height**
If your wooden fence is not as tall as you would like it to be, you can top it with some trelliswork and then grow plants over it. This is cheaper and easier than replacing the whole fence.

↗ **Trelliswork**
Traditional, wide-spaced, diamond trelliswork panels are the most popular form and perfect for most climbing plants. There are closer-spaced diamond and square options available, too.

CONTROLLING CLIMBERS

Before planting a vigorous climber, ensure that you will be able to keep its growth under control. A ladder, long-arm pruners or pruning saws may be required. Sometimes the necessary pruning can be carried out – with care – from an upstairs window to prevent growth extending into gutters or on to the roof. If you own only part of the wall, you will need to be able to prevent the climber extending to the parts of the wall that do not belong to you, since you could find yourself liable for any damage caused. Similar care should be taken to prevent damage to garden walls and the walls of outbuildings, although these are usually of less importance than main walls.

WALL SHRUBS

With a little soil space at the base of a wall – say for at least a distance 12in (30cm) out from the wall, and of similar depth before you come to foundations and footings – it is certainly possible to grow wall climbers, bedding plants and perhaps some of the smaller perennials and shrubs.

If you have twice this amount, or more, of soil coming away from the wall, then your options are even greater. With room for roots to spread under the paving, plants should have reasonable access to nutrients and moisture, and so grow larger and be easier to care for.

↗ **Tying in**
It is important to make sure that climbing plants are regularly tied in to their supports otherwise stems can stick out, flop over other plants or break, and the whole area can look untidy.

↗ **Potato vine**
The non-climbing, freestanding form of *Solanum crispum* 'Glasnevin' is a typical wall plant in that it uses the wall for shelter, not for support.

HANGING PLANTS ON WALLS

Walls and fences are useful for supporting wall pots and hanging baskets. The first tend to be under-used and are rarely seen, and the latter can often be made to look garish, with no thought given to planting that is sympathetic to the wall or building to which it is attached.

Wall pots

If the area is particularly small, then wall pots may well be the answer. These containers satisfy the desire to garden on the vertical, whilst at the same time taking up hardly any horizontal space.

They are smaller than hanging baskets and usually comprise a semi-circular container, the flat side of which is attached to the wall or fence by means of bolts and sometimes battens. They can be made of different kinds of material, from traditional terracotta to wire, metal, wood or plastic (the latter being the most lightweight). Either use trelliswork, from which the pots can be suspended, or hang the pots directly on the wall – in both cases you will also need to use eye bolts or hooks, and wires.

Hanging baskets

If colour and impact are what you want, then well-maintained hanging baskets rarely fail to impress. And the fact that they are placed at head height or above gives them a better than average chance of being noticed.

If you consider buying a ready-made basket is 'cheating', and you fancy having a go at creating your own, then all the components are available from garden centres. Making up your own basket can be hugely satisfying and you can opt for any kind of bedding plant you like. The good, old, reliable, trailing plants such as fuchsias, ivy-leaved geraniums, pendulous begonias, lobelias, ivies and nasturtiums do very well. In recent years, however, some fantastic, non-stop flowering plants, such as the Surfinia petunia, Million Bells (*Callibrachoa*), and the trailing *Bacopa* ranges have been produced. These have all been especially bred for hanging-basket growing. Once established in the container, these heavy bloomers go on, right up until the autumn frosts.

I have also used African and French marigolds, osteospermums, tobacco plants, snapdragons, sweet peas, verbenas, zinnias and the lovely black-eyed Susan (*Thunbergia*) which, when planted against a wall climbs up it, and when grown in a basket hangs down from it.

↗ Single-flower hanging baskets

Hanging baskets may be large and flowing with lots of trailing plants and with different colours, or they can be like this neat, tight, clustered ball of bicoloured pelargonium.

↗ Wall mosaics

These wall pots have been arranged into a fun mosaic pattern. They could now be enhanced by some simple planting, with a single colour scheme, or they could be left as they are.

← Hanging baskets

Even a simple, small summer hanging basket like this can transform an entrance, making it welcoming and friendly.

SMALL-SPACE TIP

It is usually a good idea to create a repeating display of wall pots, either in a row or staggered. This has the greatest impact when the planting is the same in each pot, or uses the same colour scheme.

WINDOW BOXES

Window boxes are ideal for bringing extra colour to a small garden and can be rested on sills if those on the building are large enough, or they can be fixed to the wall below windows as long as they don't interfere with any windows that open outwards.

Lightweight plastic boxes are available in various sizes and you can also buy sets consisting of the box, a water tray to avoid dripping and the all-important brackets for fixing to the wall. The planting should be carried out after the box has been put into position and secured.

Summer is when most boxes come into their own, with plants such as the floss flower (*Ageratum*), shorter snapdragons (*Antirrhinum*), bedding begonias, busy lizzies (*Impatiens*), pinks and carnations (forms of *Dianthus*), bush and trailing *Fuchsia*, *Gazania*, upright and trailing *Pelargonium*, trailing *Lobelia*, marigolds (forms of *Tagetes*) and petunias.

However, spring is also an important season and plants for a window box at this time include: *Crocus*, bedding double daisies (*Bellis*), shorter daffodils (*Narcissus*), dwarf wallflowers (*Erysimum*), forget-me-nots (*Myosotis*), grape hyacinths (*Muscari*), hyacinths (*Hyacinthus*), pansies (forms of *Viola*), polyanthus (forms of *Primula*) and tulips (*Tulipa*). For information on planting, watering and tending plants, see Chapter 10.

↗ **Window boxes**

Not enough use is made of window boxes. They are perfect for decorating the walls in a small-space garden.

↗ **Wall-top containers**

Siting a planted container on top of a wall can be most attractive, but always make sure it is secure and that it will not fall off and damage someone or something.

WALL TOPS

In a small-space garden any area for potential planting should not be ignored. Garden walls are sometimes constructed with a hollow top section that can be filled with soil in which trailing plants can be grown to great effect.

It may be possible to add such a planting area to an existing wall by building up a few courses (rows) of bricks and leaving a hollow area in the centre. This should be as deep as possible, since it will dry out quickly, and it should be filled with good-quality, fertile topsoil.

The construction of dry-stone walls means that plants can be set in pockets of soil and compost between the stones. Use compact alpines, which will thrive in these free-draining conditions, and avoid vigorous plants with strong, penetrating roots since they could undermine the stones and cause a collapse of the wall.

Sometimes you can even make use of the top surface of a wall to create an eye-catching display. Neatly clipped plants and evergreens in simple containers sitting atop a wall can be very attractive. Or you may wish to make use of a large, significant container which, when in situ on a wall, makes a bold statement. You can plant up the container whilst it is on the ground and then hoist it aloft, although it will be heavy then. Or you can put the container into its resting place and then plant it up if this isn't too awkward.

→ **Using containers**

Often there is no area of soil immediately under a wall, so the only option is to place plants in containers in such a spot. Or you could go one stage further as seen here, with a small water feature also being employed.

CONTAINERS NEAR TO WALLS

There is often no soil to speak of under a wall and it is not possible to import suitable soil to make a planting pocket. However, climbers and other plants can still be grown in containers placed against the wall. The size and weight of containers is less restricted when they are set on the ground, which allows for more ambitious planting. Make sure that the damp-proof course is not bridged, nor air vents obstructed when positioning containers.

07

OPTICAL ILLUSIONS

It's all done with mirrors

Deceiving the eye with an optical illusion – such as
a mirror – is a bit of fun. But in a small space garden
it also creates interest and gives the impression that
there is more to the space than there actually is.

↘

A BIGGER GARDEN

Although there are limits to how much you can change the physicality of your garden, it is possible, with a little know-how and careful application, to employ some optical tricks to alter its appearance. In other words, you can make your small-space garden appear bigger.

SMALL-SPACE TIP

Use either straight lines and sharp angles, or curves, circles and flowing lines in your garden – do not mix the two. A mixture of different styles can be confusing to the eye and is likely to make an area seem smaller than it really is because the eye tends constantly to be moving from one object to another, rather than following a continuous line. Similarly, stay with one style, rather than using several different types.

↘

BE CLEVER WITH COLOUR

The eye can be tricked by colour. For example, the 'hot' colours, such as the reds, oranges, pinks and yellows (of crocosmias, red hot pokers and marigolds) stand out more and appear closer, whilst the 'cool' colours of greens, mauves and blues (such as many hostas, grasses and ferns) tend to recede. Therefore, if you arrange your planting so that the hot colours are farthest away and the cooler ones are in the foreground, the colours will have a more equitable prominence.

But if you want your small space to appear larger, place the hot colours in the foreground, with the cooler colours 'receding' into the distance even if this is just a few feet away. This mimics the general landscape, where distant objects appear as bluish-grey shapes on the horizon. Similarly, plants in misty pastel shades will blur the edges of boundaries, giving the impression that the garden extends further.

PAINTED WALLS

This may actually be a small area, but because the owner has been brave, and painted the walls and supporting woodwork in a shade of lavender, the area is immediately more interesting – even if it is not to everyone's taste.

⊿ Curving road

This gently curving road is disappearing into the distance. The edges are consistently parallel and they meet at the horizon. This rule of perspective can be utilized in the garden.

⊿ Using pastel colours

This area is just 6 x 6ft (2 x 2m). Because the plants have been carefully chosen, with many pastel and pale mauve/grey/blue flowers, there is more of a perception of space and distance than if strongly coloured red, orange and yellow plants were used.

CHANGING THE PERSPECTIVE

The best example of perspective is a roadway or a set of railway tracks with parallel edges. These edges appear to come closer to each other as they recede into the distance.

You can create a false version of this by deliberately narrowing the width of a path, for example, as it extends away from the viewpoint. It makes the end of the path seem farther away than it really is. But the eye will not be deceived by this unless the proportions of the surrounding plants and objects are in keeping. So choose slightly smaller plants the farther away you get from the viewpoint. Statuary and ornamentation should also get progressively smaller. Similarly, a straight lawn can be narrowed towards the further end to make it seem longer, and using a bright splash of colour near the beginning can enhance the effect.

Objects in the distance appear smaller and in a very small plot the effect can be achieved by using just two objects such as plant pots that are identical in all but size. Place the smaller pot at the farthest point and the larger one in the foreground; the distance between them will then be exaggerated.

Also, if the plot has side walls, fences, hedges and so on, the tops can be sloped so that they decrease in height as they get farther from the viewpoint. Shaped trellises can be attached to a wall to give the impression of a distant perspective rather than a flat wall.

Overall, the manipulation of perspective tends to work from one viewpoint only and this is likely to be near to the back door or other entrance to the house. It may be a good idea, however, to select a different part of the garden as the main viewpoint, perhaps a sitting area.

TROMPE L'OEIL

This is the term used to describe an extreme deception of the eye. Whereas the manipulation of perspective and colour is relatively subtle, a trompe l'oeil is a straightforward trick, creating an illusion of something that is not there at all. Some effects are simple to achieve, while others require considerable skill. Generally, a blank wall on which to create the illusion is needed.

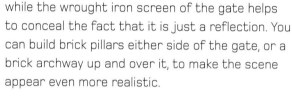

False doorways

You can create the impression of a doorway using a solid wooden door set on a wall, complete with architrave and a handle, and a pathway leading up to it. It all suggests a garden beyond the door, although it is of course entirely false.

A wrought iron gate on a solid wall will be see-through, meaning that the observer will see the solid wall behind and through the wrought iron. So put a large frost-hardy mirror on the wall first and then position the gate in front of it. This mirror will reflect the planting in the garden, while the wrought iron screen of the gate helps to conceal the fact that it is just a reflection. You can build brick pillars either side of the gate, or a brick archway up and over it, to make the scene appear even more realistic.

Using mirrors

Strategically placed mirrors are a useful way to give the impression of a larger plot. They will also increase the impact of a special feature. However, they should be put into positions where they do not immediately reflect the viewer, which would obviously give the game away.

If your garden is wide, but not very deep, you can give an impression of enhanced depth by positioning a mirror almost opposite the back door to the house, or other entrance. Then, if you surround this mirror with plants, or even some built pillar or statuary, as you step outside it will seem as if it is the way to another, hidden garden.

← Painted doorway

This attractive doorway built into a wall, with a gravel pathway leading up to it, makes you think that it can be opened and you can walk through it. But can you?

↑ Reflections

Mirrors have long been used in gardens to give an illusion of extra space. This contemporary garden effectively has a wall mirror, which from this angle reflects a part of the back wall.

FOUR SIMPLE IDEAS TO TRICK THE EYE

1. This circular hole built into a solid brick wall beckons you to go and look through it. It is so much more interesting than if the wall had continued all the way along, even if it was covered with plants. This principle does, however, rely on there being a decent view on the other side.

2. In a small space one has to have something eye-catching and interesting, but it must not take up space, or make the area seem congested. This simple wall feature makes you want to go to take a close look. And the plants can use it for support, too.

3. A semi-circular pond with a wooden path running along the flat edge gives the impression that the pond is much bigger and that it continues some distance under the path. Of course, in reality it stops just where the pathway starts.

4. We have seen how to change the perspective of a straight pathway or lawned area. However, by creating a winding pathway in a small-space garden, it feels as if you are walking a distance that is much farther than it actually is.

08

CONTAINER GARDENING

Pots of pleasure

Plants in containers can be placed in areas where there is no ground soil available to make use of every bit of available space. Of course, they will need extra care in summer in terms of watering.

THE BENEFITS OF CONTAINERS

One of the easiest ways to add colour as well as interest to any garden, large or small – and without the need for heavy garden construction – is to use floor-standing containers: troughs, pots, tubs, urns and vases (of course, hanging baskets, wall pots and window boxes all add colour but by definition these should be attached to buildings or vertical walls).

In a small-space garden, containers are especially useful because they bring life and colour, or just subtle shades of green, to corners that might otherwise remain bare. By placing pots and vases by the front door, or tubs and troughs alongside the steps to a basement garden, you are making the most of all the available space.

Floor-standing containers can be positioned on any hard surface and they are always at their best in a sunny position. If you must site them in a shady spot you have to ensure that shade-loving plants are chosen.

↗ Summer container

This classic-style vase has been perfectly planted with rose-pink *Diascia*, but it might look out of place in a modern and contemporary garden.

↙ Terracotta containers

This weathered terracotta pot is planted with a *Hydrangea macrophylla* and underplanted with hybrid *Impatiens* and variegated ground ivy (*Glechoma*) to great effect.

SMALL-SPACE TIP

It is generally accepted that the quieter, more subdued coloured containers look best: grey stone, gunmetal, or well-weathered terracotta or wood tend to provide the best backdrop for plants. If, however, the plant itself is highly architectural, such as a barrel cactus or a brightly coloured phormium, then you could opt for a ceramic container glazed in a deep blue, green or brown.

STYLES AND MATERIALS

There is an extensive range of pots, tubs, urns and vases available, made from wood, plastic, terracotta, reconstituted stone and moulded resin. The plastic ones are the cheapest but some are rather garish so look for those that are not too obtrusive. The most popular colours for plastic are white, green and brown.

There are passing fashions in all aspects of gardening, including container choice. The classic shapes, from the large Greek-style terracotta pot, the Egyptian stone urn and even the square wooden Versailles tub copied from the famous French garden, never go out of fashion. But they do look better in some garden settings than others. For example, if you live in a modern town house with contemporary architecture and furnishings, these classical-style pots would be incongruous. Much better would be to use modern steel, wood or plastic containers in square, rectangular or circular shapes.

You can be experimental as well. Try using kitchen utensils such as pots and pans, kettles and teapots, or try boots and shoes, drainpipes and even old chimney pots. Just make sure that there are drainage holes drilled into the bottom and they should be fine.

Large clay pots can sometimes look dull and uninteresting, which is why some people like to paint the sides with something colourful. Use a stencil if you are not talented with a paint brush and always use a masonry paint which is made for outdoor conditions.

↗ **Wooden containers**
Wooden tubs and barrels make useful containers and are not expensive. Use them in a country garden situation for best effect.

↗ **Stone containers**
Concrete and reconstituted stone containers in various styles are available, but be aware that these are heavy, especially once they have been planted.

→ **Terracotta basket**
This deep terracotta pot has been planted for winter colour, with *Cyclamen*, *Skimmia*, *Capsicum*, ivy and ornamental cabbage.

↘

PLANTS TO USE

Patio containers are best used for seasonal displays of annuals (mainly bedding plants) and bulbs. When in full flowering glory, they make very effective focal points.

You need not limit your choice of container plants to spring bulbs and summer bedding. If you do, your pots and tubs will look like monuments to past glories for much of the year.

Permanent plants such as small trees (dwarf fruit trees can be very successful), conifers, flowering shrubs and even some perennials, such as forms of *Hosta*, can look fabulous in containers – although they do not necessarily have the long summer of vibrant colour provided by annuals.

If you live on a chalky soil you will find that it is not possible to grow most of the plants and shrubs from the heather and *Rhododendron* family (including *Azalea*, *Camellia*, *Pieris* and many others). These are 'ericaceous' plants, meaning that they need an acid soil. The beauty of growing these permanent plants in a large tub is that you can supply them with one of the ericaceous composts widely available from garden centres.

↗ **Winter colour**
This metal winter trough has an evergreen *Azalea* at its centre; colour is provided by bright cool-weather cyclamen.

↗ **Single planting**
This simple glazed ceramic pot contains just one evergreen box plant. Simple but effective.

SMALL-SPACE TIP

Many indoor and house plants – especially those with thick or fleshy leaves – can be grown in containers outside in summer; they will add a tropical feel to your garden. You must carefully acclimatize them first by placing them in a sheltered position protected from strong sun and wind. For the first week or so it might be a good idea to cover them with a layer of horticultural fleece.

↗ Creating impact

It is not always essential to have lots of containers to create impact. Here there are a few pots, but it is the simple minimalist planting, particularly the large succulent *Aloe* in the centre, that creates the most impact.

↗ Using similar colours

If you have lots of containers of different shapes and sizes, you can unify them by planting plants of a similar style or colour. Here the gardener has created the effect using different forms of yellow and orange *Gazania*.

DISPLAYING CONTAINERS

A single specimen plant in an appropriate container can look stunning on its own. Yet many experienced gardens prefer to display containers in groups. A single plant achieves simplicity and perhaps a degree of minimalism, whereas with the latter you can create real impact, colour and glory.

Grouping containers can improve the overall effect of the display, but there are practical benefits too. It makes tending the plants easier and they benefit from mutual support. If you stagger the heights and sizes of plants you can achieve variety with a banked display. Generally it is better not to mix container styles, materials and colours within a group, as this can look like a hotch-potch affair. However, mixing can also make a statement about your individual style and this can be quite appealing.

All of these containers are, of course, ideal for standing on a patio, path, driveway or next to a door. But they can also look very good when stood in a border. Raised slightly on blocks, the container can be placed in a part of the garden that is not at its best when the plants in the tub are at their most attractive.

Do not forget, too, that containers can be used to disguise unsightly garden necessities, such as drain grills and manhole covers. Where it would be impossible to have a permanent planting over such eyesores, you can usefully place decorative containers over or on top of them.

09

THE PRODUCTIVE GARDEN

Fruit and veg

Just because a garden may be small, there is no reason why you should not attempt to grow some forms of fruits and vegetables. Tomatoes like these do not take up much space.

WHAT CAN YOU GROW?

The range of food crops that can be grown in a small space is large, but some are easier to grow than others. The main pre-requisite for vegetables and fruits (and herbs) is sunshine so if your small-space garden is quite shady the range of crops you can grow is distinctly limited.

However, if the garden area has no soil to speak of – but plenty of sunshine – you can grow almost anything, for any vegetable crop and most fruiting plants can be grown in containers. Most popular vegetables and fruits are successful grown this way, but you may find things like Jerusalem artichokes (which produce a large amount of top-growth) and asparagus (which is a long-term crop needing several years to build up to a peak of production) are not worth attempting in a container.

FRUITING PLANTS

Mid-autumn is the principal time for potting or planting fruit trees – allowing them to get their roots established before winter sets in. Which fruits to choose depends on how much space you have and what you like to eat.

If you have little available space for growing fruit trees, some smaller types can be grown in large tubs. There are two important provisos, however. Firstly, you should use as large a tub as possible, and secondly, you should only grow a tree that has been grown on a 'dwarfing rootstock'.

This means that the variety has been grafted on to special roots, which keep it dwarf (these trees are also often earlier-fruiting). The M27 rootstock will give a plant about 6ft (1.8m) high, whilst the MM106 stock will give a plant some 12ft (3.6m) high.

← Salad days
A small plot even just a few feet across and wide can be home to a useful amount of fresh vegetables.

← Fan-trained apple
In small gardens the most convenient way to grow fruit trees is to grow fan-trained trees. This apple is in full spring bloom.

TREE FRUITS

If you enjoy eating them, tree fruits can give enjoyment in both the growing and the eating. The following types are considered the most suitable for small areas.

Apples
Apple trees grow well in temperate climates. For the small garden they can be grown in compact, trained form, such as cordons or espaliers.

Pears
Make sure that any pear you grow in a container is on either the Quince C rootstock, giving plants about 8ft (2.4m) high, or the Quince A rootstock, for plants 12ft (3.6m) high. Try 'Concorde', 'Onward' or 'Williams' Bon Chretien'.

Hazel (or cob) nuts and filberts
These are closely related. They are both small trees, bearing separate male and female flowers on the same tree. The male flowers are the well-known catkins and the female flowers are small, red and unobtrusive. These trees are wind pollinated and two varieties are needed to ensure good cross-pollination. To help this process they should be in large tubs, close to one another – although the recommended distance is some 4.5m (15ft) apart. The best variety is 'Cosford'.

Citrus
Oranges (*Citrus aurantium*) and lemons (*C. limon*) and other citrus fruit can be grown in containers for the sunny patio or balcony. They will need a frost-free position in winter. The evergreen leaves and fragrant spring flowers are good enough reason to grow them and the fruits – if they develop properly and ripen – are a pure bonus.

CORONET APPLE

Apples, along with many other tree fruits, are suitable for growing in containers. If you want dessert varieties that you can pick and eat off the tree, choose self-pollinating types such as 'Falstaff', 'Greensleeves', 'Herefordshire Russet' or 'Queens Cox'. The garden centre will also stock plenty of other varieties for you to choose from. If you prefer a cooking apple, try varieties such as 'Arthur Turner', 'Lord Derby' or, of course, 'Bramley's Seedling'.

SOFT FRUITS

Unfortunately not all soft fruits are suited to containers, but you can still grow them in a small garden by having just a few canes in a sunny spot.

Strawberry

These are essential in any garden and the fact that they are small plants perfectly suited to growing in containers means that they can make a most worthwhile crop even if you have a tiny balcony. Strawberries give the quickest return of all fruits and can even carry a crop in their first year although it is not advisable, as it is a good idea to build up the plant's strength by removing flowers in the first summer after planting. There are three distinct kinds of strawberry – the summer-fruiting, the perpetual (or remontant), and the alpine strawberries. They all prefer a warm, sunny, sheltered position, which usually guarantees the best-flavoured berries.

Raspberry

There are two types of raspberries – those that fruit in the summer and those that are ready in the autumn. The summer varieties have quite a short season, but they do produce high yields. The autumn types on the other hand will bear fruits from the end of summer through to the first frosts. Raspberries will not like a light, dry soil. Instead, for best results, they need a really moisture-retentive soil packed full of goodness, from well-rotted manure to garden compost.

Blueberry

These are one of the best fruits for containers because they need moist, acidic soil, with a pH of 4.5–6.0, which is rarely found in garden soil.

→ **White currants**
White currants grow as a framework of branches emanating from a single stem; this is the variety 'White Versailles'.

They are deciduous bushes which are perfectly hardy, although late spring frosts can kill the flowers, which will impact on the fruiting potential. Blueberries are self-fertile, but you will get a better crop if you have space for two plants. Always use rainwater for watering.

Red, white and blackcurrant

The most often seen of these is the blackcurrant. It needs a deep, fertile soil and produces fruit on wood grown during the previous year. Among the best cultivars are 'Ben Lomond' and 'Ben Arek'.

Red and white currants are more tolerant of a wider range of soils and conditions. The fruits are borne of shoots that develop from a framework of branches emanating from a single stem and cropping is best on plants that are two or more years old. 'Stanza' and 'Red Lake' are the best of the red cultivars, whilst 'White Versailles' is the best of the whites.

↑ **Strawberry fruits**
Strawberries are arguably more successful when grown in containers than directly in the garden soil; slugs are less of a problem and the fruits do not rot on wet ground.

VEGETABLES IN A SMALL SPACE

Huge encyclopaedias on vegetables have been compiled and here we have only a few pages so we will focus just on the most popular types for the small-space gardener.

Let's start off, however, by looking at one popular and successful way to grow temporary vegetable crops in a small space.

↓ Sweet peppers

If you do not have enough space for a dedicated kitchen or vegetable garden, consider growing some of the more 'attractive' vegetables, such as sweet peppers, in the flower border.

GROWING BAGS

Unlike most fruits (with the exception of strawberries), temporary vegetables can be grown with great success in growing bags. When these were introduced in the 1970s they revolutionized tomato growing, and growing in containers generally. They are, quite simply, polythene bolsters of peat, coir or recycled composted products, sometimes with sand or bark added. These days, too, you will often find that the compost in the bags has been impregnated with fertilizers to help the plants during the first few weeks, or pesticides to ward off the major insect pests, as well as the increasingly important, water-saving gel granules.

Although growing bags are mainly used for cultivating tomatoes, they are also very suitable for peppers, aubergines and cucumbers, plus hardier vegetables such as lettuce, onions, beetroot, radish and even French or dwarf beans. Strawberries can also do very well in them. The bags can be placed outside in a sunny place or can be sited in a greenhouse for early crops or greenhouse-recommended varieties of tomatoes, peppers, aubergines and cucumbers.

The planting process is very straightforward. Start by placing the bag into its permanent position, in a greenhouse or at the base of a sunny wall, and then cut it open. Most bags have printed on them the ideal places for making the cuts, and this will depend on whether you are growing tomatoes, peppers and aubergines (typically three plants per bag), cucumbers (two), or strawberries (six to eight).

Loosen the compost within the bag if it appears to be compacted, and water it if it seems to be dry. Remove the plants from their pots and plant them as evenly as possible along the centre

↑ Tomatoes in growing bags

In a standard-sized growing bag there is sufficient room, and volume of compost, to accommodate three cordon tomato plants.

of the bag. To stake them special supports are available for holding bamboo or plastic canes. These are essential for cordon and vine tomatoes (but not trailing tomatoes), aubergines, the larger types of pepper and cucumbers.

Vegetable crops are usually quite demanding in their nutrition intake, so you must provide food on a regular basis. Indeed, it is not a bad idea to water the plants in with a weak solution of liquid feed when planting. Then for summer plants, you will need to feed them every week or ten days as there are only limited supplies in the bag.

Use a tomato feed for all the fruiting plants (including peppers, aubergines, cucumbers, strawberries) as this contains slightly greater amounts of potash.

SMALL-SPACE TIP

It can be difficult to tell when growing bags need watering. The simplest test is to press a piece of newspaper on to the compost in the bag. If it picks up water the bag is moist enough. If not, a drink is needed!

SALAD PLANTS

These are arguably the most appropriate vegetables for a small garden. They are short-term crops enabling you to have a succession of crops on the same piece of ground and, with the exception of tomatoes, the plants are all generally quite small. Salad plants are also easy. Along with rocket and spring onions, here are the mainstay vegetables to grow:

Lettuce

During spring sow lettuce seed very thinly, ½in (1cm) or so deep, either in containers or directly in the garden soil. When they are planted out, or thinned out if sown outside, they should be around 1ft (30cm) apart; or 6in (15cm) apart if you are growing the popular loose-leaf variety 'Salad Bowl'. Slugs can be a problem with lettuce, so choose your preferred control measure (bait, beer-pubs, or the various biological nematode controls). Always water lettuce in the morning as watering in the evening increases the chance of disease.

↓ Lettuce leaves

There are many types of lettuce available. In a small garden, it is a bonus if it is also attractive to look at. The variety shown here is green and purple 'Salad Bowl'.

← Cherry tomato

This variety, known as 'Gardener's Delight' is a cherry tomato, which is a heavy cropper, and plants do not get as big as some of the larger 'beefsteak' varieties.

Tomato

These, to my way of thinking, are every bit as crucial to a salad as green leaves. Without the tomato about three-quarters of all savoury dishes would be missing a vital – and colourful – ingredient. If you do not have a greenhouse for sowing seed of tomatoes in spring, it is usually better to buy young plants from the garden centre or by mail order.

Three to a standard growing bag is usual, or if you have space to plant them in the soil, set them about 16in (40cm) apart.

Sweet pepper and chilli

Mid-spring is the time to sow these, in a shallow pot, kept on a bright, warm windowsill or in the greenhouse. Without these facilities, buy young plants in spring. If sowing, prick out the seedlings into small pots or modules of sowing compost. Keep warm at 12–25°C (54–77°F) and plant them out in early summer.

VEGETABLES IN LARGE CONTAINERS

Most vegetables and salad plants can be grown in large containers. Place them in a sunny position and pay particular attention to watering and feeding. You should also be aware, when putting the containers into position, that you will need to gain access to them at harvest time.

PEAS AND BEANS

The 'pod and seed' vegetables are full of vital vitamins and minerals. They can roughly be divided into those that produce edible seeds (peas and broad beans) and those that are grown for their edible pods (runner beans and mangetout peas). The pods of French or dwarf beans can be eaten, or just the seeds from within them. All can be grown in containers, but the larger the container you can use, the better.

Broad or Fava beans

These are probably the best of the family in large pots or tubs. They are easy to grow and will even germinate on a piece of damp newspaper! Broad beans are very hardy, extremely prolific and top of the list as nutrition providers. Sow the beans outdoors in autumn or spring 9in (23cm) apart. Harvest them from mid-summer onwards, picking them while they are still young and tender.

Garden peas

When picked straight from the pod these are so sweet that they can be eaten raw as a snack. They are often described as round or wrinkled – not a precise description of the shape of the pea, but more as a way of classifying them as hardy (round for autumn sowing) or tender (wrinkled for spring sowing). Sow them straight outdoors in late autumn or early spring, depending on the variety, setting them 1–2in (2.5–5cm) deep and 2–3in (5–7cm) apart. Harvest them around 12 weeks after sowing.

Mangetout and sugar snap peas

These are bred to be eaten whole, pod and all. mangetout (French for 'eat all') are ready when the pods are flat, before the peas inside have

developed. Sugar snaps should be eaten once the peas are fully developed and the pods have rounded out. Sow and harvest as above.

French or dwarf beans

The taller climbing beans are especially useful for smaller gardens, as they can be grown to scramble up an arch in a flower border. They are also prolific! In fact, the more you pick them, the more they will grow. Haricot beans are the dried, mature bean seeds; flageolets, the tender, delicately flavoured beans so popular in France, are actually the half-ripe, shelled bean seeds. Sow outdoors in spring where they are to grow.

Runner beans

These have been a staple in our diet for many generations. Dwarf varieties are especially suited to exposed gardens as they are less affected by wind than the taller climbers. Sow in individual pots in the greenhouse in mid-spring, or outdoors 6in (15cm) apart in late spring after all frosts have finished. Picking should start approximately 12 weeks from sowing.

→ **Broad beans**
These can be grown in containers and, as they are some of the smallest members of the pea and bean family, they are also good for growing in the soil of small-space gardens.

SMALL-SPACE TIP

The roots of runner beans go down a long way, so a deep container with well-rotted compost or manure in the base is essential. For this reason also, the more successful crops are usually grown in well-prepared garden soil. If you want a really good crop, the soil should be prepared about six months beforehand!

ROOT CROPS

These include crops such as potatoes, carrots, beetroot, parsnips, turnips and swedes. They are perfect for the low-water garden, as they do not generally need supplementary watering (being relatively large-rooted plants the all-important moisture-absorbing root hairs are down where the water is!).

Potatoes

These are by far the most frequently grown vegetables. I thoroughly enjoy nipping out to dig up a plant to find 20 or 30 healthy, clean tubers. They can be cooked and eaten within the hour and the taste can be out of this world. The only downside to growing potatoes is that they can take up quite a bit of space. Doing it properly, you would need to space 'first early' varieties every 12in (30cm) or so in rows some 24in (60cm) apart, and a bit more than this for the 'second earlies' and 'maincrops'.

First early varieties should be planted in early spring, for harvesting in summer. Second early varieties are planted up mid-spring for lifting in mid-summer, and maincrop varieties are planted in late spring; lifting can take place in mid-summer for using immediately, or you can wait until early autumn for lifting and storing, which means that they can be used in the winter.

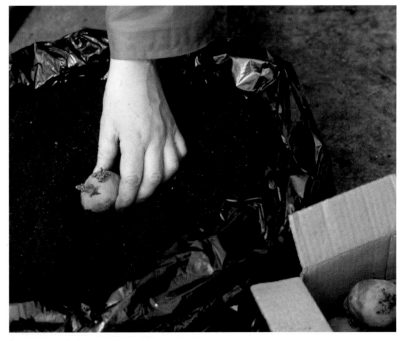

↗ **Potatoes in black bags**
Those who only have a patio or balcony space can still grow potatoes – by growing them in black bags, or special potato bags that are available today.

SMALL-SPACE TIP

Garden centres offer potato 'bags' these days, but you can simply use a thick black bin liner. This means you can grow potatoes even on a patio or balcony. Just make sure that the bag is rolled up or sealed in the recommended way and that you add more soil or compost as the plants grow, to keep the tubers in the dark.

↗ **Onion pot**
Onions make a good crop for containers, and as they do not take up too much space you can grow a good number per container.

Carrots

These are very easy to grow. All carrots require is a soil that is not too stony and not freshly manured. Otherwise they are not too demanding of time and expertise. Carrot root fly is the only problem a gardener growing them is likely to come across; unfortunately there are no chemicals to control this fly, so if your crop is susceptible it is recommended to put up a barrier around the plants, about 2ft (60cm) high, as the flies do not generally fly above this height.

↘

THE ONION FAMILY

The onion family is very large, for not only does it include salad, pickling, red and white onions of many different sizes, it also includes chives, shallots, garlic and leeks. In all cases you can sow seeds, but for shallots you usually plant the small bulbs, which multiply over the growing season. Leeks comprise a long, stem-like collection of rolled leaves, unlike any other vegetable and, it has to be said, not much like onions either. None of the onion family is difficult to grow, but they are all quite different in their growing techniques.

↗ **Carrot 'Chantenay Red Cored'**
Standard carrot varieties like these do not take too much space to grow but if you are growing them in containers it is better to go for the round, stump-rooted varieties.

BRASSICAS

These include such luminaries as cabbage (spring, summer, autumn and winter varieties), cauliflower, broccoli and calabrese, Brussels sprouts and kale. They are very valuable additions to any vegetable plot and they also have the benefit of not being particularly thirsty vegetables. They make good container subjects, but because of their size, you cannot usually get many in a tub. Turnips and swedes, being root crops and therefore very different in habit and shape to their 'green' cousins, are not usually thought of as brassicas. But they are, and just as susceptible to all of the foibles and weaknesses of the main members of the family – such as vulnerability to the fungal disease clubroot and prone to attack by birds.

↘ Cabbage
Cabbages (and all members of the Brassica family) are suitable for containers, but because of their size you will be limited to the number you can grow. Shown here is the variety 'Hispi'.

HERBS AND SPICES

Most herbs, including parsley, tarragon, chives, rosemary, thyme and mint, do well in containers. In fact, I only ever grow mint in containers as all forms are vigorously invasive and will grow into other nearby plants. Growing them in a container keeps them under control. I have had great success also with a small hanging basket containing nothing but parsley – when hung up next to the back door it made 'harvesting' much more convenient.

↑ **Herb garden**
With a decent amount of space, a formal herb garden can be both aesthetically pleasing and productive as well.

↗ **Herb wheel**
For those with just a small area, a herb wheel is an attractive option, with different species growing between the spokes.

↗ **Mixed herb border**
Many herbs, including lavender, sage and bronze fennel as seen here, can be grown mixed with ornamental plants in a border.

1.0

TYPES OF PLANTS AND THEIR CARE

Flower border

It is all very well putting out a few plants you like the look of, but for a flower border to look as colourful and floriferous as this, you will need to know how to look after them as well.

↘

ANNUALS, BIENNIALS AND BEDDING PLANTS

There is often confusion about these terms, but it's actually very simple. Annuals are plants that are sown, grow, flower and die all within a year, whereas biennials are sown and grown on in one year, and flower and die during a second year.

The term 'bedding plant' is generally used to describe plants of either type, but that are usually grown in quantity and planted in 'beds', for a massed display. These include bedding geranium (*Pelargonium* spp), the marigold (*Tagetes* spp), *Petunia* spp, the fibrous-rooted bedding begonia (*Begonia semperflorens*), polyanthus (hybrids of *Primula* x *polyantha*), sweet Williams (*Dianthus barbatus*) and many others.

All of these plants are important to small-space gardens, as they do not grow large and they provide huge amounts of short-term colour for vivid seasonal displays.

Planting

Tender annuals and bedding plants should not, of course, be fully planted out in the garden or in containers until all danger of frosts has passed. The soil in which they are to grow should be prepared well; before planting, fork the soil over, making sure that any annual weeds are completely buried. Perennial weeds should be removed as these will re-grow if left.

These plants will be growing and flowering quickly, and continuously, throughout summer, so they will be hungry and need plenty of food. To get them off to a good start, sprinkle a handful of general fertilizer evenly over the soil, following the manufacturer's instructions.

While the plants are still in their trays or pots, give them a thorough watering. If the bedding plants are in individual pots or strips, gently remove them. Try to do as little damage to the roots and stems as possible. Place them in a hole dug with a trowel The hole should be the same size as the pot. Firm them in place with your hands and water them in.

↗ **Shop bought**
These winter pansies have been bought from a garden centre and they have come in white polystyrene trays.

↗ **Position with care**
Carefully position bedding plants before digging the hole, so that you are certain they will make the best display.

↗ **Firm them in**
Using your hands, firm the plants in place, and then water them in.

↗ Bedding and containers

All bedding plants – whether they are annual or biennial by nature – are suitable for providing short-term colour in containers. Here, blue polyanthus and yellow pansies combine for a bright, late-winter pot arrangement.

BULBOUS PLANTS

Bulbs are essentially fleshy modified leaves enclosing an embryonic flower – which means that when you buy a bulb you can almost guarantee that it will flower. Popular examples are *Narcissus, Lilium* and *Nerine*.

Tubers and corms are also often described as 'bulbs', and this can cause confusion with gardeners. All three types are basic storage organs for the plant, containing a supply of water and food that keeps the plant alive while it is dormant; however, most tubers and corms are also modified, swollen stems. New shoots emanate from buds at the tops of the organs. *Begonia* and *Dahlia* are good examples of tuberous plants, whilst *Gladiolus* is the best example of a corm plant.

A rhizome, however, is a fleshy underground stem that acts as a storage organ, and perhaps the best examples here are the border *Iris*. Each year the rhizome produces buds and shoots from the end, so the older part dies and shrivels.

Planting

Plant out bulbs out as soon as you can, labelling the place to avoid any accidental damage. The spring-flowering bulbs are the first to be planted during the 'bulb year' and should be planted in the autumn. Daffodils and other forms of *Narcissus* could be planted in late summer or beginning of autumn, as they produce roots early.

The majority of bulbs, with the exception of tulips, can be planted as soon as the summer bedding has been removed or when the ground is vacant. In the case of tulips they should be planted from mid-autumn onwards; too early, and any emerging new growth may easily be damaged by frost.

↗ **Bulb planter**
Here a special bulb-planting tool, which removes a core of soil, is being used.

↗ **Aid drainage**
Most bulbs are damaged by very wet soil, so it is a good idea generally to sit the bulbs on a layer of sand, which drains water away from the vicinity of the bulb.

↗ **Firm with your foot**
Place the bulb in the base of the hole, replace the core of soil, and gently tread it firm.

Summer-flowering bulbs, such as gladioli and dahlias, are planted in the spring. These two, and many other types of summer bulb, are tender, and will need lifting or otherwise protecting in the winter. Lilies can be set out in the autumn.

As a general rule, however, a bulb should be planted so that there is as much soil above it as the height of the bulb itself. Exceptions are bluebells and daffodils, which should be planted to twice their own depth. Always ensure the base of the bulb is in contact with the ground. Air pockets result in the roots failing to develop.

↓ **Daffodil clump**
There are few more welcome sights in the garden than cheery daffodils on a late-winter or spring day.

PERENNIALS, ALPINES, FERNS AND ORNAMENTAL GRASSES

Although not woody in nature, these plants will survive from year to year and provide you with colour and interest. In most cases after four or five years you should lift the plants out of the ground and split, or divide them, and then replant them. This not only stops the plant from getting too large and cumbersome, but also gives it a new lease of life and you some more plants.

Planting

Ideally, perennials should be planted either in the spring or autumn. Water the plants in their pots thoroughly an hour or two before planting them, especially if the weather is hot, dry or windy.

If you do end up buying a potted perennial that is pot-bound, at planting time gently tease out as many of the roots from the congested 'ball' of root as possible, but try not to damage them too much. Dry roots bought in packs can be soaked in a bucket of water for a couple of hours before planting them in the soil, or potting them.

It is a good idea to set out the plants in a bed or border whilst they are still in their pots. This will give you an idea of what the eventual display will look like. It is all too easy to plant perennials too close to each other; this can result in the plants being more susceptible to attack by fungal diseases and it can lead to weak growth.

When planting, dig a hole that is large enough to accommodate the entire root system. Carefully remove the plant from its container and, if possible, spread out the roots as you place the plant in the hole. Set the crown of the plant at soil level, then back fill and firm gently, taking care not to damage the roots. The final act is to water the plant in.

← Mixed border

A border that contains perennials and bulbs – with perhaps space for some annuals and maybe a small shrub or two – is referred to as a 'mixed border', and can be a real joy at the peak of flowering.

↗ Planting a hosta

This hosta, a perennial, is being planted. First you should dig the hole, then carefully remove the plant from its pot.

↗ Firm in position

Place the rootball of the plant in the hole, making sure it is not set too deep. Then firm it in position with your hands and water it in.

↗ Mulching

Here, the soil around the hosta is being mulched using commonly available cocoa-shells. Mulching with this looks neat, conserves water, prevent weeds and, in the case of this particular material, offers a lovely chocolate smell for a week or two.

↘

TREES, SHRUBS AND CLIMBERS

There will be few trees being bought and planted in the average small-space garden, but as we have seen so far in this book, there are plenty of shrubs that are suitable and many forms of climbing plant.

Planting

Although bare-root trees, shrubs and climbers are available for much of the year, late autumn is the ideal time for planting them, and this is when nurseries and garden centres will be stocked to capacity with them.

For the vast majority of trees, shrubs and climbers the soil needs to be free-draining, but moisture-retentive. If your soil is sandy and does not hold water well, you must incorporate plenty of humus into it before planting. This can be provided in the form of well-rotted garden compost or animal manure. Similarly, if your soil is heavy clay and water does not easily penetrate it, your plants will need organic matter to retain moisture. Mix the organic matter into the soil around and within the planting hole; do not plant any plants directly into organic matter as it is too strong for the fine root hairs and will burn them. Before you plant your container-grown plants, break up the surrounding soil and the base of the hole first. Firm the plant in position and water it in.

↗ **Take out a hole**
Planting a laurel: take out a hole twice as wide and deep as the pot the plant came in.

↗ **Add planting mixture**
Put some planting mixture (sold in bags from the garden centre) into the hole. This will help the plant's roots to establish.

↗ **Check roots**
There should be a nice amount of healthy roots in the pot, but any more than this and the plant will be pot-bound, meaning it could take longer to establish in the soil.

Just before you set the plants in the ground, apply a handful of bonemeal fertilizer over the area. Work it in to the surface of the soil, using a hoe or rake, tread the area firm and then rake it level.

Staking

Small trees need supporting with a stake – even if you are planting them in a secluded, sheltered courtyard, for only a little wind is required to make an unsupported plant lean. The stake should be driven into the hole before planting, to avoid damaging the plant's roots. The top of the stake should come up just to the base of the first outward branches, to avoid unnecessary chafing.

Climbers

Climbers need to be planted against a wall, or fence, wires or trelliswork, some 12in (30cm) away from the supporting structure. Make the hole and lay the plant's roots in the hole, but angle the stem of the plant so that it is pointing towards the wall. Arrange the roots in the hole so that they are pointing away from the wall to where the soil will generally be moister.

In all cases, water the plants in, and throughout the first few years check them regularly for dryness, particularly during hot weather (see below).

↗ **Check depth of planting**
Make sure the plant is not set too deeply. Place a cane over the rootball and adjacent soil – they should be the same height.

↗ **Firm the plant in**
Firm the plant in place with your foot – but try not to damage the roots. The final act will always be to water it in.

SMALL-SPACE TIP

When choosing trees, shrubs or climbers at the garden centre do not be swayed by a display of flowers. Examine the plants to determine their states of health. Make sure their stems are healthy and strong, with no damage or disease.

TENDING PLANTS

All plants need a certain amount of care and attention during the year if they are to give the best displays for our pleasure, and small-space plants are no exception. Feeding and watering are by far the most crucial requirements, but pruning is also an important element.

Watering

It is important never to allow plants to dry out completely. Even sun-loving cacti and succulents need water to survive; it is just that they take in the little bit of moisture that is available and then store it.

Once you have planted up your small space, watering is essential until the new plants have become established – and this could take two or even three years. Even then you should always water your plants during hot and dry spells. It is best carried out either early in the day or in the evening – both are times when the sun is low in the sky and evaporation will be at its slowest. Remember also, a good soaking of the soil every few days is better for plants – and less wasteful of water – than a mere splash around the leaves and stems twice a day!

It is both economically and environmentally sensible to save as much natural rainwater as possible, and the commonest way to do this is to install a water butt. Rainwater, from roof run-off, carried via guttering and downpipes, can then be collected in the butt.

Towards the bottom of the butt there is a tap, so that you can easily fill a watering can. Although you cannot rig a hosepipe up to a water butt, you can fill countless cans of water and, if you live on a water-metered property, this will save a significant amount of money.

↗ Watering by hosepipe
On-going aftercare of newly planted plants is crucial, and the single most important thing to ensure is that the plants do not dry out.

↗ Using a water butt
If you have the room, a water butt can be invaluable – it saves money on your water bill, and is good for the environment.

Mulching

In any garden, even the smallest, mulching is of great importance, especially where the conditions are dry and the soil full of roots – such as under drying walls or large trees. A mulch is a layer of organic (or inorganic) material applied around plants and on top of the soil surface. It has many benefits, from moisture retention in the soil, to weed control and winter protection of the roots.

The various materials used typically include homemade compost and leafmould, bought-in farmyard manure and bark, as well as stone chippings, gravel and even decoratively coloured crushed glass. Fabric and plastic sheet mulches can also be deployed, but these are ugly so are best confined to use in large plantations and commercial nurseries.

Organic matter is ideal if you want to feed the soil and increase its moisture-retaining capabilities. Manure from horses and pigs is most commonly available, usually from farms which put up signs, but sometimes a town-based garden centre will be able to order it in for you. It is not particularly expensive and produces luxuriant plant growth but it is heavy and does not prevent weed growth.

Feeding

Plants growing in a small-space garden may actually need more feeding than those growing in the open garden. This is for several reasons. Firstly, nearby walls and buildings will create shade and put plants under a degree of stress, so it is important to make sure that they get a regular supply of nourishment from the soil.

Secondly, some plants may be reluctant to flower if they are growing in the shade. This can, in part, be helped by providing fertilizers that are proportionately higher in potassium such as tomato or rose fertilizers, which are designed to promote flowering.

Thirdly, a small area is more likely to be home to plants in containers and these need more feeding (and watering) than plants growing in the open ground. The best course of action is to provide annual mulches of manure in early spring (see left). Between mulches, it is a good idea to supplement the feeding by applying granular or pelleted chicken manure, which is strong, effective and easy to apply – if a little smelly at first. Also in spring, inorganic balanced fertilizers, such as Growmore, can be applied according to manufacturers' recommendations.

↗ Mulching with bark
Mulching, here using shredded bark around a rhododendron, is good practice.

↗ Applying fertilizer
A springtime feed of a general fertilizer, in this case a granulated blood, fish and bone mixture, will help your plants to stay healthy.

Pruning

In a small garden, you need either to select and grow plants that will achieve a modest size when fully developed, or to ensure that you limit the size of larger subjects by keeping them under control. In other words, pruning them carefully so that they do not grow too big for the space allocated to them.

Pruning is also undertaken to maintain a plant's shape and habit, to remove dead, damaged, or diseased growth, and to improve the flowering, fruiting and foliage display. Awkwardly placed shoots will upset the balance of a plant and such growths should be cut out. Shrubs that have grown out of balance can be reshaped if these general guidelines are followed: first, remove straggling branches to a shoot or bud within the main bulk of the plant; second, carefully but systematically reduce the number of growths on the 'good' side of the plant; third, cut back weak shoots hard and strong shoots lightly on the 'bad' side of the plant; fourth, feed the plant with a good general fertilizer; and fifth, mulch with compost or manure.

Plants that are not maintained – that is, pruned regularly or at least annually – can often become a dense mass of tangled branches. This means that the shoots in the middle of the mass are deprived of light and air, and are prone to dying back. During windy weather the stems can rub together, causing injury to themselves and the branches they are rubbing against. All of these conditions lead to a greatly increased risk of disease.

Always cut to a healthy bud, making the pruning cut some ¼in (6mm) or so beyond it; any more than this and the extra piece of stem beyond the bud will die, which can then spread down into living plant tissue.

Staking and supporting

Many herbaceous plants that re-grow annually will require some form of support to prevent them flopping over other plants, or in on themselves. Tie them to bamboo canes, or buy purpose-made wire hoop supports that are pushed in the ground for the plant to grow up and through. These should be put in position in the early to mid-spring period, before the plants start growing apace.

Some shrubs may also require additional support, using stakes or stout canes as they grow. Trees should have their stakes planted with the plant, rather than have the stake planted subsequently, as this can damage the roots under the soil. Check tree ties every few months and loosen them if they are beginning to constrict the stem or trunk as it grows.

Climbers need to be trained to trelliswork. As new stems on these plants develop, they should be tied in to their supports, to avoid wind damage. If this is done regularly, they should be in position to replace any older wood that can be pruned out at the appropriate pruning time. Left untied they may break, get in the way (of a path or patio, for example), or at least become inflexible enough to make tying in later on more difficult.

← Staking and tying trees

This deciduous *Spiraea* 'Gold Flame' is being pruned in spring, to encourage it to produce masses of new shoots, each carrying decorative golden leaves.

Deadheading

All cultivated flowering plants need deadheading – the removal of faded flowers before the plant has created the seed which follows. By doing this you are saving the plant from a huge amount of wasted energy; it will also either encourage more flowers in the same year, or help to build up the plant for better flowering the following year.

With woody plants use a pair of secateurs, cutting off the faded flowers, removing the stalks down as far as the first set of leaves.
As always there are exceptions. Rhododendrons, for example, should have their old flowerheads snapped off, using your fingers. Bedding plants and some soft perennials can be deadheaded and this may be best done with fingers, or a pair of shears (as you would with, say, heather). Bulbs, such as daffodils, are deadheaded by pinching off the swollen seed sac, which forms just under the faded flower.

At the end of the growing year a perennial border should be tidied up. Old, dying top-growth should be cut back to ground level (unless the seedheads are required for winter decoration). Try to remove stems as close to the crown of the plant as possible.

↖ Provide support
Supporting tall perennials, such as delphiniums, is important if you want the flower spikes to stand upright – it may in fact stop them from snapping off altogether in a high wind.

↖ Tying in climbers
Climbers and wall shrubs (this is a form of *Lavatera*) should be tied in regularly to their supports.

← Deadheading with fingers
Deadheading (here with a *Rhododendron*) is important as it can prolong a flowering period, or encourage better flower the following year.

1.1.

A–Z DIRECTORY OF PLANTS FOR SMALL SPACES

Houseleeks
This small-rosette form of Sempervivum will
be ideal for a small, sunny border or container.

HOW TO USE HARDINESS ZONE MAPS

Before investing time, effort and, of course, money on new plant purchases, you should first understand your geographical location and what this means to the plants in your care. It is particularly important to have an appreciation of temperatures and the tolerance of plants to cold.

Just because you may, by necessity, need to choose smaller plants because you have a small garden, do not for one minute believe that the plants are any more or less hardy than their larger counterparts. Small plants are just as vulnerable to damage from freezing temperatures and icy blasts of wind as big plants. The exception to this is, arguably, the alpine range of plants; these do not mind cold temperatures, but they do hate prolonged wet soils.

Generally, therefore, any plant needs to be chosen with care if you live in a cold area, or your garden is especially exposed to the elements. But fortunately there is some benefit to plants

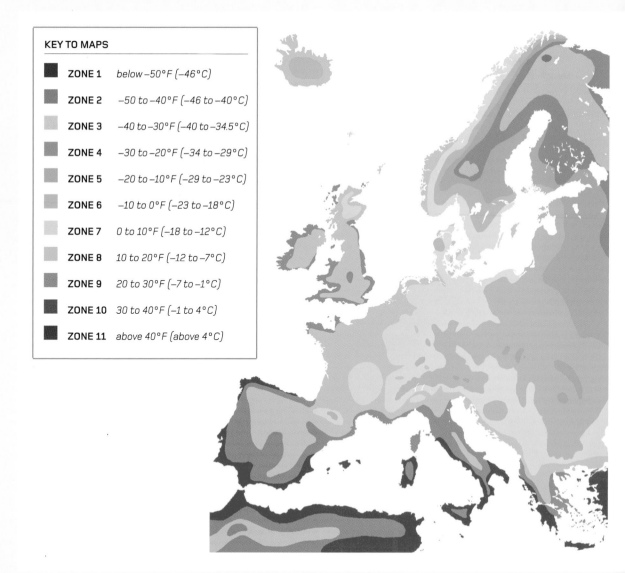

KEY TO MAPS

■	**ZONE 1**	*below −50°F (−46°C)*
■	**ZONE 2**	*−50 to −40°F (−46 to −40°C)*
■	**ZONE 3**	*−40 to −30°F (−40 to −34.5°C)*
■	**ZONE 4**	*−30 to −20°F (−34 to −29°C)*
■	**ZONE 5**	*−20 to −10°F (−29 to −23°C)*
■	**ZONE 6**	*−10 to 0°F (−23 to −18°C)*
■	**ZONE 7**	*0 to 10°F (−18 to −12°C)*
■	**ZONE 8**	*10 to 20°F (−12 to −7°C)*
■	**ZONE 9**	*20 to 30°F (−7 to −1°C)*
■	**ZONE 10**	*30 to 40°F (−1 to 4°C)*
■	**ZONE 11**	*above 40°F (above 4°C)*

growing in many small-space gardens, for these areas will be sheltered and warmer (possibly taking the form of enclosed courtyards).

It is worth remembering, also, that new plants are being developed all the time and often it is hardiness, and other weather tolerances, that is bred into them.

Therefore it is useful to know, when buying your plants, which climate suits them best – the parts of the world in which they originated

usually dictate this – but it is not exclusively the case. If you live in Europe or the US, the maps on these pages will give you an indication of the plant hardiness zones for where you live. And as you will see from the Directory section which follows, plants for a small-space garden are quite adaptable, so wherever you live you should be able to find a selection of good plants that suit you and your garden's requirements.

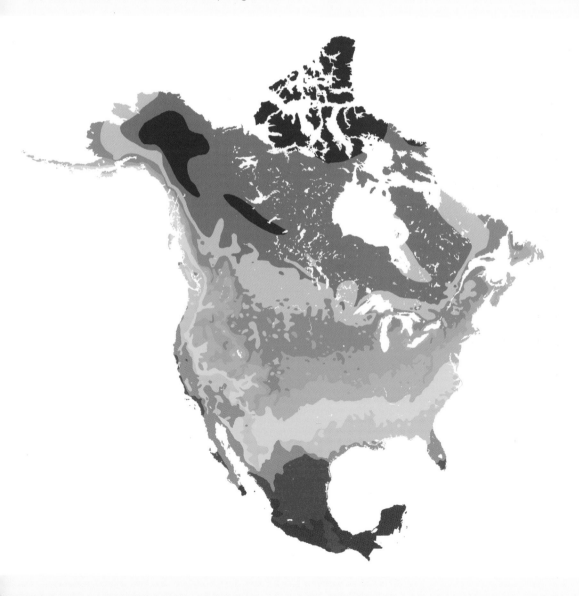

GOOD PLANTS FOR SMALL SPACES

This part of the book will help you when you are choosing the plants to grow in your small-space garden. Sadly we cannot offer you an exhaustive compendium of every plant appropriate to the smaller garden. Also, note that I have intentionally omitted trees, and specialist and hobby plants – such as alpines, dwarf conifers, miniature roses and even bonsai trees. Although these plants, and others like them, are entirely appropriate in a small garden, whole books have been written about them and we simply do not have the room in this book to cover them in sufficient detail.

Therefore, on the following pages I have selected some of those plants that have worked well for me in small spaces over the years, and also a few that give a really good account of themselves, making them very worthwhile plants for the small amount of space they use.

Plants are listed alphabetically within the section that relates to their type (annuals, bulbs, perennials, trees and shrubs and so on). For each plant, the following information is provided:

Origin: This tells you, if known, where the species was discovered. Understanding which country or part of the world a plant comes from, and the average climate or even altitude, can help you to understand the plant's growing requirements and the conditions it prefers.

Type: This refers to the 'type' of a plant – for example, whether it is grown from a bulb as opposed to a tuber, corm or rhizome, or whether it is an annual (grows, flowers and dies within one year) or a biennial (the same but in two years), or perhaps a shrub rather than a climber.

USDA zone: These are the climate zones referred to on pages 118–119. The zone numbers quoted here, based on UK Royal Horticultural Society data, are on the cautious side, so if you are not prepared to take any chances, follow the hardiness ratings to the letter. But raised beds, good drainage, sheltered gardens and those with a sunny aspect, all give plants a better habitat – so there is plenty of scope for experiment.

Height and spread: This will be useful when choosing and designing plants for a garden. All sizes are given for plants at maturity.

Description: Here you will discover generalized details of the plant's shape, size and habit, along with flower and foliage colour and shape.

Popular species and varieties: Sometimes a plant species will exist without offspring or siblings. It will therefore have a relatively small entry in this book. But with, for example, the *Primula* genus, there are hundreds of species and cultivars (abbreviation of 'cultivated variety'), and so there will be many to recommend.

ANNUALS, BIENNIALS AND BEDDING PLANTS

Ageratum 'Adriana Nova' F1

Begonia semperflorens 'Focus Mixed'

AGERATUM (*Floss flower*)

ORIGIN: Central and South America
TYPE: Annual
USDA ZONE: Z10
HEIGHT AND SPREAD: 6–12in (15–30cm)

DESCRIPTION: Soft flowers from powder blue to pink or white are held in compact, long-lasting clusters. This is one of the most popular of summer annuals for edging a bed or border, but it's good for containers as well.

POPULAR SPECIES AND VARIETIES: *Ageratum houstonianum* 'Blue Danube' AGM is 6–8in (14–20cm) high, with lavender blue flowers until mid-autumn. 'Blue Mink' has flowers that are a distinct mid-blue, 'Adriana Nova' is deeper and 'Album' is white.

BEGONIA SEMPERFLORENS (*Bedding wax begonia*)

ORIGIN: South America
TYPE: Tender perennial grown as an annual
USDA ZONE: Z9–11
HEIGHT AND SPREAD: 7–16in (17–40cm)

DESCRIPTION: Often referred to as the fibrous-rooted begonias (because the other popular types emerge from bulb-like tubers), this group of hybrids and cultivars have bronze to green leaves. Flowers of white, pink or red, up to 1in (2.5cm) across, bloom continuously outdoors in summer. Some varieties have single or double blossoms, some quite large, whilst others have numerous clusters of small flowers.

POPULAR SPECIES AND VARIETIES: The 'Focus' range has attractive bronze leaves and white flowers with yellow stamens. 'Two Tones' comprises a mixture of bicolours each with dark bronze and green foliage – the 'two-tone' effect. Look for the 'politicians' series: Ambassador Series, Senator Series and President Series – all are particularly good bedders.

Brachycome iberidifolia 'Purple Splendour'

Celosia Plumosa 'Century Fire'

BRACHYCOME IBERIDIFOLIA (Swan River Daisy)

ORIGIN: South Australia
TYPE: Half-hardy annual
USDA ZONE: Z8
HEIGHT AND SPREAD: 8–18in (20–45cm)

DESCRIPTION: Noted for its long season of flowering (throughout summer and into autumn, until the frosts arrive), brachycomes are easy to grow, thriving in a dry and sunny position. They are good in containers, as well as in the front of mixed flower borders. They seem to be particularly 'at home' when they are planted amongst roses.

POPULAR SPECIES AND VARIETIES: 'Purple Splendour' produces masses of purple-blue heads, whilst 'White Splendour' (crisp white) is perfect as an accent plant in a border. 'Summer Skies' is a mix of sweetly scented, pretty pastel shades, and 'Dwarf Bravo Mixed' is a cushion-forming, compact mix of dark and light blue, violet and white, each flower possessing either a black or yellow centre.

CELOSIA ARGENTEA (Cockscomb/'Prince of Wales' Feather)

ORIGIN: Tropical and sub-tropical Asia, Africa and America
TYPE: Hardy annual
USDA ZONE: Z9
HEIGHT: 8–24in (20–60cm)
SPREAD: to 18in (45cm)

DESCRIPTION: These plants make eye-catching displays when used in garden bedding schemes, or they make fine specimen pot plants for a greenhouse or conservatory. The flowers come in dense plumes.

POPULAR SPECIES AND VARIETIES: *Celosia argentea* is divided into two groups: the Plumosa types, which are best for bedding out, and the Cristata types that have crested flowers and make better pot plants. If this type is bedded out and the summer is wet, water can rest in the flattened flowerheads, causing them to rot. The Plumosa Century Series, of which 'Century Fire' is one of the most vibrant-coloured forms, is the best for bedding. *C. spicata* has slender flower spikes and can also be used as cut flowers; look for 'Flamingo Feather' with pink blooms.

Clarkia amoena Satin 'Deep Rose'

Erysimum 'Citrona Orange' and 'Citrona Yellow'

CLARKIA AMOENA (Godetia)

ORIGIN: California
TYPE: Hardy annual
USDA ZONE: Z9
HEIGHT: to 24in (60cm)
SPREAD: 12in (30cm)

DESCRIPTION: This plant is now called *Clarkia amoena*, but the old name of *Godetia* persists; in fact, it has practically become the common name. It is a free-flowering plant all summer and is easily grown in a light soil and in full sun. It is very suitable for cutting. Set plants out at a distance of 18in (45cm) from each other.

POPULAR SPECIES AND VARIETIES: Look for 'Deep Rose' (a deep pink), 'Thoroughly Modern Millie' (a combination of soft and rich pinks, reds and salmon with attractive azalea-like blooms), 'Rembrandt' (carmine-rose and white) and 'Charivari' F2 (a mixture in shades of pink, peach, coral and white).

ERYSIMUM CHEIRI (Wallflower)

ORIGIN: Southern Europe
TYPE: Perennial sub-shrub usually grown as a hardy biennial
USDA ZONE: Z7
HEIGHT: 10–18in (25–45cm)
SPREAD: 10–16in (25–40cm)

DESCRIPTION: Used for spring bedding, wallflowers also make good pot plants for a cold or slightly heated greenhouse or conservatory. Sow seed in a nursery bed in late spring or early summer. Bare-rooted plants are available in the autumn for immediate planting. Space plants 8–12in (20–30cm) apart.

POPULAR SPECIES AND VARIETIES: Mostly sold in mixtures, including 'Persian Carpet Mixed', and 'Treasure F1 Mixed' (a modern, vigorous, branching, early flowering variety). Of the single colours available, look for 'Fire King' (rich scarlet), 'Blood Red' (magenta), 'Mayflower' (cream yellow) and the 'Citrona' range, of which orange and yellow are by far the best. The Siberian wallflower (*Erysimum x allionii*) AGM reaches a height of 12in (30cm) and is very much like the bedding wallflower; flowers are either golden or orange.

Impatiens 'Cranberry Punch Mixed'

Lobelia erinus 'Little Gems Mixed'

IMPATIENS (*Busy Lizzie*)

ORIGIN: Globally, except South America, Australia and New Zealand
TYPE: Tender perennial, designed to be grown as an annual
USDA ZONE: 10
HEIGHT AND SPREAD: 6–14in (15–37cm)

DESCRIPTION: These are low-growing, partly shade-tolerant yet highly floriferous bedding plants, looking their best from early summer until the autumn frosts. They come in a variety of colours from white and pale pink through to oranges, deep reds and near purple.

POPULAR SPECIES AND VARIETIES: The 'Cranberry Punch Mix' is particularly free-flowering, and comes in shades of pink and red. The 'Super Elfin' series of F1 hybrids, to 10in (25cm), is available in individual colours, such as 'Lipstick' (rose pink), 'Salmon Blush' (peachy salmon) and 'Velvet Red' (deep red). The 'Accent Bright Eye' series has flowers of more than 2in (5cm) across.

LOBELIA ERINUS (*Edging, annual or trailing lobelia*)

ORIGIN: North America
TYPE: Annual
USDA ZONE: Z9
HEIGHT AND SPREAD: 4–8in (10–20cm) when grown upright, but can trail 12in (30cm) or more

DESCRIPTION: Bedding lobelias are grown for their blue, purple, crimson and white flowers. They are a great favourite for borders, although they are demanding, needing a humus-rich and moist soil. Those sold as having a trailing habit can be planted to trail from a hanging basket or tumble over a patio container.

POPULAR SPECIES AND VARIETIES: 'Cambridge Blue' AGM (mid-blue) and 'Mrs Clibran Improved' (deep blue with a white eye) both grow to 4in (10cm) in height, whilst 'Little Gems' comes in purple and white. 'Cascade' AGM is an excellent trailing variety in a wide colour range. Many of the newer *Lobelia* hybrids have been bred to vary the length of the stems and to extend the colour range.

Matthiola 'Ten Week Stock' (pink)

Mesembryanthemum bellidiformis 'Gelato Red'

MATTHIOLA INCANA (*Ten-week stocks, Brompton stocks*)

ORIGIN: Man-made hybrids from parent plants originating in southern Europe
TYPE: Half-hardy annual
USDA ZONE: Z6
HEIGHT: 8–24in (20–60cm)
SPREAD: 12in (30cm)

DESCRIPTION: These plants flower throughout summer and are grown equally for their bright, colourful flowers and their powerful scents – so important in a small-space garden. Stocks thrive best in a good, well-drained soil in a sunny spot. Space the plants 1ft (30cm) apart. Place short sticks or brushwood between plants soon after planting out, for they are liable to be flattened by rain when in flower. Use in beds for cutting and amongst other summer plants.

POPULAR SPECIES AND VARIETIES: The summer-flowering 'Dwarf Ten Week Mixed' has bright, double and very sweetly scented flowers in a similar range of colours. 'Brompton Mixed' is a variety for overwintering, flowering from late spring onwards; it is also one of the most fragrant. 'Cinderella Mixed' possesses a huge colour range from cream and dusky pink through to lavender and purple.

MESEMBRYANTHEMUM BELLIDIFORMIS
(*Livingstone daisy*)

ORIGIN: Man-made hybrids from parent plants originating in South Africa, particularly the Cape Peninsula
TYPE: Half-hardy annual
USDA ZONE: Z9
HEIGHT: 4–6in (10–15cm)
SPREAD: to 12in (30cm)

DESCRIPTION: This plant flowers profusely in sunny weather and comes in many glistening colours. It is ideal for rock gardens and for the front of a flowerbed. Space plants 12in (30cm) apart.

POPULAR SPECIES AND VARIETIES: The common name has also become a varietal name: *M. bellidiformis* 'Livingstone Daisy' produces a brilliant array of pinks, whites, magentas, oranges and creams which open with the sun. 'Lunette' is lemon yellow with a deep orange-red centre, whilst 'Gelato Red' is a deep, almost metallic, peachy pink.

Pelargonium 'Decora Red' (ivy-leaved and trailing)

Pelargonium 'Flower Fairy White Splash'

PELARGONIUM (Bedding geranium)

ORIGIN: Man-made hybrids from parent plants originating mostly in South Africa, but some species come from tropical Africa, the Middle East and Australia

TYPE: Tender perennial grown as an annual
USDA ZONE: Z10
HEIGHT: 3–40in (8–100cm)
SPREAD: 3–24in (8–60cm)

DESCRIPTION: The pelargonium is one of the most popular summer-flowering plants. Given a sunny position it will grow in most soils, but should be watered during dry periods. It flowers extremely freely throughout summer until cut down by autumn frosts. The ivy-leaved pelargoniums are best in hanging baskets and window boxes. In all cases, remove dead blooms regularly. Occasional liquid feeding in summer will encourage free-flowering. Plants can be lifted before autumn frosts commence, potted up and overwintered in light, frost-free conditions, watering sparingly. They can be pruned back in early spring.

POPULAR SPECIES AND VARIETIES: There are hundreds of different varieties and the names may vary from country to country. The following, however, is a representative sample. Mop or ball-head singles: 'Venus' F1 (white with rose-red eye and a picotee edge), 'Black Magic Appleblossom' F1 (pink and white apple blossom flower, set off by striking dark leaves) and 'Black Magic Red' F1 (rich red flowers above velvety, almost black foliage). Multiflora (branching stems producing more, slightly smaller flowers): 'Avanti Apricot' F2 (apricot pink with a small white eye) and 'Scarlet Eye' (rose pink fading to white). Trailing ivy-leaved: 'Summer Showers Burgundy' (burgundy flowers) and the 'Decora' range in red, pink and white.

Petunia 'Ramblin Mixed'

Petunia Colour Bells 'Bavaria Bell'

PETUNIA

ORIGIN: Man-made hybrids from parent plants originating in tropical South America

TYPE: Half-hardy annual

USDA ZONE: Z7

HEIGHT: 6–16in (15–40cm)

SPREAD: to 36in (90cm)

DESCRIPTION: Petunias bloom throughout summer, until cut down by frosts. They thrive in full sun, but can tolerate a little dappled shade for a small part of the day. Set out young plants 12–18in (30–45cm) apart when frosts have finished. They are amongst the best plants for window boxes and other plant containers, but can also be used amongst other summer-flowering plants in beds and borders. Some forms are highly scented.

POPULAR SPECIES AND VARIETIES: There are many dozens of cultivars. Of the Multiflora types, which have single and double flowers up to 3in (8cm) across, and excellent weather tolerance, two of the best are: 'Celebrity Bunting' F1 (red, white and blue mix) and 'Ramblin Mixed' F1 (pink, lilac, pale blue and white). Of the Grandiflora types, which have frilly doubles and dramatic, trumpet-shaped flowers up to 5in (13cm) across, some of the best include 'Sundance Mixed' (masses of cream-white, red, blue, ruby and salmon flowers), 'Blackberry Fool' F1 (rose purple) and 'Banana Milkshake' F1 (creamy yellow and white).

BULBS

Anemone blanda 'White Splendour' and 'Atrocaerulea'

ANEMONE BLANDA AGM (*Windflower*)

ORIGIN: North America, Europe, Asia
TYPE: Rhizomatous and tuberous perennial
USDA ZONE: Z4–8
HEIGHT AND SPREAD: 6in (15cm)

DESCRIPTION: Mainly woodland plants, there are a great many species and cultivars of *Anemone*, ranging from 6in (15cm) to 4ft (1.2m) in height, and flowering variously from early spring to late autumn. *Anemone blanda* AGM grows from tubers and is available in shades of white, pink and blueish purple. It has open, daisy-like flowers, which can appear even in mid-winter, but it is normally at its best in early spring.

POPULAR SPECIES AND VARIETIES: Garden centres usually sell these plants in mixed pots or packets, but occasionally you will find named varieties. Those to look out for include 'Radar' AGM – the oldest and the best – a bright magenta, daisy-like bloom with a white centre, 'Charmer' (a clear pink), 'White Splendour' AGM (large, pure white flowers) and its counterpart, the rich purple 'Atrocaerulea'. Also growing from tubers, *Anemone coronaria* is very popular, mainly in the form of two strains descended from this species – the De Caen Group (often known as the Poppy Anemone) and the St Brigid Group. Colours range from deep blue and purple shades, through to red, pink and white. The St Brigids come in semi- or double-flowering forms. Tubers are usually sold in mixes; however, several named varieties are available, including 'Hollandia' (scarlet, single) and 'Lord Lieutenant' (deep blue, double). All of these are good as cut flowers.

Colchicum autumnale AGM

Colchicum speciosum 'Atrorubens'

COLCHICUM AUTUMNALE (Autumn crocus)

ORIGIN: Central and western Europe
TYPE: Perennial corm
USDA ZONE: Z5
HEIGHT AND SPREAD: 4–10in (10–25cm)

DESCRIPTION: One of the most dramatic of autumn flowers, colchicums are crocus-like, which is confusing, especially as the common name is 'autumn crocus'. However, these two plants are not related. Colchicums arise, leafless, in late summer and early autumn and give a wonderful display of flowers. The leaves follow in late winter, long after the flowers have faded. When in full leaf, colchicums are large and can smother smaller plants. They can look unsightly in a border when dying back, so you are advised to choose their position with care. They are also poisonous.

POPULAR SPECIES AND VARIETIES: *Colchicum autumnale* AGM produces masses of lilac-pink, goblet-shaped flowers – and all from a single corm. 'Alboplenum' is white, double and produces three to five flowers from each bulb. 'The Giant' has rose-lilac flowers on 10in (25cm) long stalks; each flower has a white base. If you prefer something a little less showy, then there is the single, white cultivar 'Album'. *C. speciosum* 'Atrorubens', a vivid sugar pink, whilst 'Waterlily' AGM has purple-lilac double flowers.

Crocus tommasinianus 'Ruby Giant'

Crocus oliveri subsp. *balansai* 'Zwanenburg'

CROCUS

ORIGIN: Mid- and southern Europe, Middle East, central Asia and northern Africa
TYPE: Perennial corm
USDA ZONE: Z4–8
HEIGHT: 4in (10cm)
SPREAD: 1–3in (2.5–7.5cm)

DESCRIPTION: The *Crocus* is one of the true harbingers of spring and is among the best known and most popular of all the early blooming, bulbous plants. Most forms are easy to grow, free-flowering and increase well in suitable conditions. There are over 80 species and whilst many can be grown in our gardens, those most likely to be found are cultivars. Despite flowering early, weak sunshine in mild weather will encourage them to open their flowers wide, making a very colourful show.

POPULAR SPECIES AND VARIETIES: Often sold as mixed colours, the Dutch crocus are arguably the best of the garden forms. There are still plenty of named, single-colour cultivars to choose from, including the silvery lilac-blue 'Vanguard', the pure white 'Jeanne d'Arc', the rich purple-violet 'Queen of the Blues' and 'Pickwick' with its striking, purple-striped blooms. *Crocus tommasinianus* AGM is one of the first to flower, in late winter and early spring. Its soft lavender flowers are small and slender. There are a number of varieties. Look for 'Whitwell Purple' (purplish blue) and 'Ruby Giant' (deep purple). Crocus in the Chrysanthus group are free-flowering. Growing to around 3in (7.5cm) in height, they are at their best from late winter to early spring, depending on conditions. Look for 'Cream Beauty' AGM (soft creamy yellow), 'Snow Bunting' AGM (white), 'Blue Pearl' AGM (delicate blue with a bronze base and silvery blue on the outside of the petals) and 'E.P. Bowles' (clear yellow flowers, feathered with purple on the outside). *C. sieberi* subsp. *sublimis* 'Tricolor' AGM is very distinctive, with lilac blooms, each possessing a large, yellow throat and broad white band.

C. kotschyanus AGM comes into its own in early autumn, when its pale lilac, yellow-throated blooms appear. Finally, in late autumn, the saffron crocus (*C. sativus*) comes in to bloom; its large purple flowers have three deep-red stigmas that are the source of the spice saffron.

Bright golden yellow and brown flowers are produced by the excellent *Crocus oliveri* subsp. *balansai* 'Zwanenburg'.

Cyclamen hederifolium AGM

Cyclamen coum AGM

CYCLAMEN

ORIGIN: Southern Europe and the Mediterranean
TYPE: Tuberous perennial
USDA ZONE: Z6–9
HEIGHT: 4in (10cm)
SPREAD: 2–4in (2–10cm)

DESCRIPTION: Although most people think of cyclamen as winter-flowering pot plants, the hardier (yet more delicate-looking) outdoor forms are both graceful and extremely useful plants for growing in shady spots under trees. But you don't have to grow them under a tree; they make a colourful carpet in any small area and they seem to positively thrive on dappled to heavy shade and dryness at the roots.

POPULAR SPECIES AND VARIETIES: The most often-seen types are forms of *Cyclamen coum* AGM that is at its best from mid- to late winter. The pointed buds open to light or dark pink, or white. Most have rounded leaves with lovely silver and green patterning in the top and plain dark red on the underside. Although the plants themselves are tough, the leaves can easily be damaged by a severe frost. Similar in appearance is *C. hederifolium* AGM which flowers in late summer. The first flowers often appear just after rainfall and blooms always appear before the leaves. There are both pink and white forms. A great attraction of the plant is the varied shapes and the marbling, blotches and silvering of the leaves – none are ever the same. Other *Cyclamen* suited to a small garden include *C. repandum* (beautiful, reddish-purple turned-back petals in spring), *C. libanoticum* AGM (large, clear pink flowers in spring), *C. cilicicum* AGM (pink in autumn), *C. cilicium f. album* (white in autumn) and *C. graecum* (the pink flowers of which are held well clear of heavily marbled foliage).

Eranthis hyemalis AGM

Galanthus nivalis AGM

ERANTHIS HYEMALIS AGM (Winter aconite)

ORIGIN: Southern Europe
TYPE: Rhizomatous perennial
USDA ZONE: Z5
HEIGHT: 2–4in (5–10cm)
SPREAD: 3–4in (7.5–10cm)

DESCRIPTION: The buttercup-yellow aconites are a cheery sight in late winter. The cup-shaped flowers, supported by collars, or 'ruffs' of green, deeply toothed bracts, distinguish these from other winter plants such as hellebores and snowdrops; they are like nothing else and every garden should try to make room for one or two of them.

POPULAR SPECIES AND VARIETIES: Mainly you will find the straight winter aconite (*Eranthis hyemalis* AGM); it will seed itself if the conditions are right, and may in time form a large carpet of late-winter colour. *Eranthis x tubergenii* has larger blooms and the form 'Guinea Gold' AGM is rather more vigorous.

GALANTHUS NIVALIS AGM (Common snowdrop)

ORIGIN: Western Europe
TYPE: Bulbous perennial
USDA ZONE: Z4–6
HEIGHT: 4–10in (10–25cm)
SPREAD: 2–3in (2.5–7.5cm)

DESCRIPTION: With their nodding white flowers, snowdrops are one of our favourite winter-flowering bulbs. There are many species and cultivars, but the common snowdrop (*Galanthus nivalis* AGM) is the most widely grown form. It produces its finest show in a fertile soil in partial shade. The blue-grey leaves are flat and strap-shaped; the white flowers have small green markings on the central sets of petals.

POPULAR SPECIES AND VARIETIES: 'Flore Pleno' AGM is a double form, and among the named varieties look for 'S. Arnott' AGM, which is slightly scented, and 'Viridapicis' with a green spot on both the inner and outer petals. 'Lady Elphinstone' has yellow markings. *G. elwesii* AGM is often called the giant snowdrop. Its broad, grey-blue leaves accompany the large flowers on 10in (25cm) high stems. The blooms have three long petals and three shorter ones with bright green markings.

Narcissus bulbocodium

Narcissus cantabricus

NARCISSUS (Daffodil)

ORIGIN: Southern Europe, northern Africa, western Asia, China, Japan
TYPE: Bulbous perennial
USDA ZONE: Z4–6
HEIGHT AND SPREAD: 3–18in (7.5–45cm)

DESCRIPTION: Ask anyone to name 'spring flowers' and most will come up with the daffodil within the first two or three suggestions. Few plants epitomize more the essence of spring – and the promise of warmer days ahead – than the daffodil. Its golden-yellow trumpet flowers, many with a delicate, evocative perfume, can really brighten up a dull spring day. And, in fact, many of them technically bloom in late winter, too. Daffodils comprise the biggest single group of spring bulbs. They are the hybrid forms of large and trumpet-flowered narcissus and botanically the plants are quite complex. Of course, all most of us really need to know is when it will flower, what colour it will be and, for those of us with only a small amount of space to play with, how large they will become! The packs that are sold in garden centres are generally displayed by colour, which means that if you would like some whitish daffodils you can go straight to them very easily. But while you're looking at them you might be swayed by some cream, double or even brightly coloured daffodils.

POPULAR SPECIES AND VARIETIES: My favourites, in no particular order, are 'Dutch Master', large, deep golden flower, excellent in pots, 16in (40cm) high; 'Mount Hood', broad, white petals with an ivory white trumpet, great for planting in lawns, 18in (45cm) high; 'Merlin', pure white petals with a delicate, bright yellow cup edged in orange red, 16in (40cm) high; 'Rip Van Winkle', a double yellow, dwarf variety (some liken it to a loose dahlia flower), 5in (13cm) high; 'Tahiti', golden-yellow, double flowers with bright orange-red parts between the petals, 15in (38cm) high; 'Hawera', two to six cream-yellow, slightly fragrant flowers appear per stem, 8in (20cm) high; 'February Gold', golden yellow and early, one of the all-time best, 12in (30cm) high; 'Tete-a-Tete', golden yellow, multi-headed, long lasting and dwarf, one of the best for pots, 6in (15cm) high; and *Narcissus bulbocodium*, the hoop petticoat daffodil, golden-yellow flowers with narrow, pointed petals, 3–6in (7.5–15cm) high. *N. cantabricus* is similar – a delightful little plant with near-white blooms.

Nerine bowdenii AGM

NERINE BOWDENII AGM

ORIGIN: South Africa
TYPE: Bulbous perennial
USDA ZONE: Z8–9
HEIGHT: 18–24in (45–60cm)
SPREAD: 5–6in (12.5–15cm)

DESCRIPTION: You cannot fail to be impressed by the flowers of these autumn bloomers. Several species of *Nerine* are half hardy, which means that they will need protection from cold in winter, but the exception is *Nerine bowdenii* AGM. This can be grown in a sheltered spot, ideally at the foot of a sunny wall. The long-lasting, bright pink flowerheads appear before the foliage. Each tall stem carries up to 12 blooms with undulating petals. Plants can be left undisturbed for several years. All other nerines are best grown as pot plants and brought under cover for winter. Nerines flower best when the plants are well established in the soil or in their containers. For the first year or so, the newly planted bulbs may look a little thin, with just one or two flower stems. After this, however, plants get going and can be prolific – lasting for two or even three decades.

POPULAR SPECIES AND VARIETIES: *Nerine bowdenii* 'Alba' has white flowers, whilst 'Pink Triumph' has arguably the best pink flowers of any of the 30 or so commonly available cultivars. The Guernsey lily, *N. sarniensis* AGM, produces bright scarlet flowers on 18in (45cm) stems. Due to its vibrant colouring it has been used to produce some very worthwhile hybrids. *N. flexuosa* is not as tall, growing to 12in (30cm), but it produces lovely pink umbels. Each bloom has narrow, reflexed and crinkled petals. There is also a white form available listed as 'Alba'. Another nerine on the tender side is *N. undulata*. Each flowerhead comprises up to 12 mid-pink flowers, with narrow, wavy (or 'undulating') petals. *N. filifolia* is virtually evergreen; it throws out new grass-like leaves as the old ones fade. In autumn these leaves provide a backdrop to the heads of small, bright pink to white flowers.

Scilla mischtschenkoana AGM

SCILLA MISCHTSCHENKOANA AGM *(Squill)*

ORIGIN: Russia, Iran
TYPE: Bulbous perennials
USDA ZONE: Z5–6
HEIGHT: 2–4in (5–10cm)
SPREAD: 2in (5cm)

DESCRIPTION: Between mid-winter and mid-spring these plants produce a veritable carpet of pale blue; there is a deeper blue stripe on each petal. It grows to 6in (15cm) in height and, like so many bulbs, is best planted in groups. The scaly bulbs are perennial and slowly extend by producing offsets. Unlike most early bulbs they do not require a thorough baking during summer, instead preferring a slightly damp spot, especially once the leaves die down. These plants seed themselves freely, and you can easily allow a colony to build up by letting them self-sow.

POPULAR SPECIES AND VARIETIES: Arguably the best-known family member – *S. siberica* AGM – follows *S. mischtschenkoana*, with lovely blue, nodding flowers. *S. sibirica* is the loveliest and easiest species; its leaves make their appearance in early spring and are soon followed by the 4in (10cm) stems carrying three or four blue, bell-shaped flowers. *S. sibirica* 'Spring Beauty' is a robust form with larger bright blue flowers. 'Alba' is a good white-flowering variety. *S. verna* has electric-blue flowers in spring. And the dainty *S. bifolia* AGM produces two strap-shaped leaves which open out to allow a 4in (10cm) high stem, holding blue star-shaped flowers, in late winter. 'Rosea' is a purple-pink form and 'Alba' is white. *S. puschkinioides* is a Central Asian species with pale blue or white star-shaped flowers; the leaves are quite long and thin, with a white central stripe.

PERENNIALS

Achillea 'Feuerland'

Carex. oshimensis 'Evergold' AGM

ACHILLEA MILLEFOLIUM (Yarrow)

ORIGIN: Throughout the Northern Hemisphere
USDA ZONE: Z2
HEIGHT: 24–28in (60–70cm)
SPREAD: 18–28in (45–70cm)

DESCRIPTION: Yarrow is a difficult-to-control lawn weed, but the decorative perennial types have been bred for flowerheads which bloom for a long period from late spring until early autumn. These heads can be loose clusters or flat heads, but they are all comprised of a mass of tiny, daisy-like flowers. Colours range from white through to the deepest red.

POPULAR SPECIES AND VARIETIES: 'Alabaster' is pale yellow, fading to white; 'Bloodstone' is very deep red; 'Cassis' is a deep cherry red; 'Fanal' (sometimes found as 'The Beacon') opens bright red and fades to brownish yellow; 'Feuerland' (or 'Fireland') opens to bright red orange, fading to orange and yellow. Even smaller at 12–24in (30–60cm) in height is the Summer Pastels Group, a mixture of colours – not always pastels – from white, pink and yellow to orange and red.

CAREX (Sedge)

ORIGIN: Worldwide, especially the temperate and Arctic regions
USDA ZONE: Z5–7
HEIGHT: to 39in (100cm)
SPREAD: 6–10in (15–25cm) or even indefinite in the case of pond sedges

DESCRIPTION: These are generally densely tufted, grass-like plants (they are not actually members of the grass family), but there are some forms with a looser habit and creeping underground rhizomes that you should avoid in the smaller garden. Forms of the large *Carex* genus are grown primarily for their foliage, even though the flowers are quite significant. Male and female flowers are carried separately, but on the same stem; the female ones resembling little brown cones. Many of the kinds available have foliage that is essentially brown; this tended to be ignored by gardeners a hundred years ago, but with the subtler styles enjoyed by today's gardeners, these plants have become very popular.

Carex elata 'Aurea' AGM

Helleborus orientalis

POPULAR SPECIES AND VARIETIES: The most popular form is *C. elata* 'Aurea' AGM, known as Bowles' golden sedge. Its golden leaf colouring always looks its best when sited in full sun, although it will tolerate some dappled shade. Look also for *C. oshimensis* 'Evergold' AGM, which produces dense, evergreen clumps of deep green leaves each with a broad, central stripe of cream to yellowish white; *C. conica* 'Snowline', which has narrow white margins to deep green leaves; and *C. saxatilis* 'Ski Run', which has contorted leaves striped with white – just 4in (10cm) high.

HELLEBORUS (Hellebore)

ORIGIN: Western and central Europe, Russia
USDA ZONE: Z3–6
HEIGHT: 12–36in (30–90cm)
SPREAD: 12–24in (30–60cm)

DESCRIPTION: The winter-flowering hellebores are addictive, such is their magic, especially the hybrids of *Helleborus orientalis*. Most hellebores will grow in full sun or light shade, but at all costs you should avoid growing them in places that are exposed to cold winds.

POPULAR SPECIES AND VARIETIES: Christmas and Lenten roses are two widely known common names, but these are by no means the only members of the family. The Christmas rose (*H. niger* AGM) has flat, pure white flowers, occasionally with pinkish tones. The most popular hellebores, however, are those classified under *H. x hybridus* (the Lenten rose and the Orientalis Hybrids), with a great many named varieties in a wide range of colours from almost black to purple, yellow, pink and white, some with plain flowers, others spotted and veined.

Hosta fortunei var. *aureomarginata* AGM

Hosta 'Patriot'

HOSTA (*Plantain lily*)

ORIGIN: Japan, China, Korea
USDA ZONE: Z3
HEIGHT: 1–36in (2.5–90cm)
SPREAD: 10–48in (25–120cm)

DESCRIPTION: Hostas are grown principally for their handsome foliage, which is produced in a range of shapes, sizes and colours. In summer the plants produce strong stems with mostly trumpet-shaped flowers, varying from pale lilac or mauve to white. Leaf size is very variable, from those with huge affairs 12in (30cm) or more across and long, to the small-leaved types of just 2in (5cm). The variegated forms are often the most popular with cream, white, gold and blue markings on the leaves.

POPULAR SPECIES AND VARIETIES: There is plenty of choice for the gardener as more than 1,000 cultivars and varieties exist. *Hosta venusta* AGM is tiny, with a height of just 1in (2.5cm) but it has a ground-covering habit giving it a total spread of some 12in (30cm). Its leaves are mid- to dark green and its trumpet-shaped, purple flowers come in profusion in late spring. *H. sieboldiana* is a variable plant making a 24in (60cm) tall mound, with large, oval leaves with rippled edges; the colours vary from mid-green to deep blue green. *H. ventricosa* AGM produces bold, shiny, dark green leaves and purple summer flowers. *H. ventricosa* var. *aureomaculata*, meanwhile, has spring leaves that are splashed with gold in the centre, but be warned that they revert to all-green by summer. Look out also for *H. fortunei* var. *aureomarginata* AGM with splendid variegated foliage, and the cultivars 'Bright Lights' (leaves of mid-green with a darker blue-green edge) and 'Golden Tiara' AGM (a fast-growing hosta with green-centred leaves, edged with gold).

Iris 'Arctic Fancy' AGM

Iris reticulata 'Harmony'

IRIS

ORIGIN: Temperate regions of the Northern Hemisphere
TYPE: Rhizomatous and bulbous iris
USDA ZONE: Z5–10
HEIGHT AND SPREAD: 4–36in (10–90cm)

DESCRIPTION: There are two main types of iris – those growing from bulbs (which are not covered in this book as they are more frequently grown as alpine plants) and others grown from rhizomes. These include the flamboyant bearded iris that provide colour in early summer, have stiff, sword-shaped foliage and grow best in full sun. Mostly we grow the hybrids, of which there are many, with newcomers continually being added to the already formidable lists. Such is the range of colours and combinations that it is best to look for them in springtime at a garden centre, or to study an iris specialist's catalogue.

POPULAR SPECIES AND VARIETIES: The dwarf bearded irises are excellent for the small-space garden, or the front of a border or sunny pocket on the rock garden. Their heights range from 4–12in (10–30cm). They are fully hardy and are available in a wide range of colours. 'Lacy Snowflake' is one of the brightest, purest white flowers. A semi-dwarf bearded iris is 'Blue Denim', with lovely mauve-blue flowers. The intermediate bearded irises include 'Arctic Fancy' AGM with mauve-blue and white flowers and 'Honeyplic' AGM with cream, white and honey-brown flowers – both of these plants reach 18in (45cm). The tall bearded types include *Iris germanica* AGM, often referred to as purple flag or London flag. In late spring and early summer they produce scented blooms with rich purple falls and a white beard; the standards are of light purple. It grows to between 24–36in (60–90cm), depending on the variety. Although it is not a bearded iris, the winter-flowering Algerian iris, *I. unguicularis* AGM, is a real beauty. Dwarf bulbous iris include the spring-flowering *I. danfordiae* (deep yellow), *I. histrioides* 'Major' AGM (rich blue), and *I. reticulata* 'Harmony (sky blue and royal blue, with yellow-rimmed white blotches).

Phlox subulata 'Bonita'

Primula sieboldii

PHLOX

ORIGIN: North America
USDA ZONE: Z3–6
HEIGHT: 4–48in (10–120cm)
SPREAD: 8–30in (20–75cm)

DESCRIPTION: There are very small perennial phloxes and there are some very large ones (and some decorative annual types as well). All are free-flowering plants, perfect for the 'cottage garden' style.

POPULAR SPECIES AND VARIETIES: Most border phloxes are from the species *Phlox paniculata,* which typically grow up to 48in (120cm) in height. Look for 'Juliglut' (sometimes labelled as 'July Glow') with flowers of a strong rose pink and one of the first to flower in mid-summer. 'Mount Fuji' AGM is later-flowering, right into mid-autumn and its outstanding free-flowering and robust nature combine with the purity of its white flowers to make an unbeatable perennial. *P. subulata* is an evergreen, mound-forming perennial just 4in (10cm) high and with a spread of twice this. Masses of star-shaped, white, pink or mauve flowers appear in early summer. Look for 'Bonita' (pale lilac) and 'Marjorie' (rose pink).

PRIMULA (*Primrose*)

ORIGIN: Throughout the Northern Hemisphere, southern South America
USDA ZONE: Z5–6
HEIGHT: 2–32in (5–80cm)
SPREAD: 2–24in (5–60cm)

DESCRIPTION: The *Primula* genus ranks as one of the largest and most variable, durable and likeable of all plant genera. There are primulas for growing in pots, on rockeries, in flowerbeds, in woodland dells and at the sides of a pond. Slightly shaded places are best and they prefer a fairly rich, organic and slightly acid soil.

POPULAR SPECIES AND VARIETIES: There are masses of alpine primulas and just as many larger perennial forms, too. Sitting somewhere in the middle is *Primula sieboldii,* with a height of some 12in (30cm) and a spread of 18in (45cm). The Gold Laced Group produces flowers of a dark red to deep chocolate brown, with each petal edged in golden yellow; it's a stunning plant for a cool, damp spot in part shade. The common or wild primrose (*P. vulgaris*), makes a fine addition to a small border, but is perhaps most at home in a wild area in longish, uncut grass.

Pulmonaria 'Roy Davidson'

Pulmonaria saccharata 'Mrs Moon'

PULMONARIA (Lungwort)

ORIGIN: Europe
USDA ZONE: Z3–6
HEIGHT: 8–12in (20–30cm)
SPREAD: 12–24in (30–60cm)

DESCRIPTION: In addition to lungwort, the *Pulmonaria* genus also goes by the common names of the Good Friday plant, thunder and lightning, soldiers and sailors, and Jerusalem sage. The small, five-petalled flowers are familiar in spring gardens and the typically spotted leaves make a pleasing addition to shady borders later on. There are ten species, all of which are small herbaceous plants with short flower stems. The oval or oblong foliage may be green or marked with silvery spots and blotches and is usually roughly hairy, like all parts of the plant.

POPULAR SPECIES AND VARIETIES: *Pulmonaria saccharata* is an attractive plant from France and Italy and has large leaves that are heavily spotted and leafy flower stems with purplish blooms. The best cultivars are those with the most silvered leaves, which include the 'Argentea Group' AGM. *P. angustifolia* AGM has plain, pale green leaves, which emerge early and contrast well with the mid-blue flowers. Its cultivar 'Munstead Blue' has light green, unspotted leaves and bright blue flowers. Two first-class hybrids are 'Roy Davidson' (narrow leaves, lightly spotted in silver; its flowers are mid-blue fading to pink) and 'Mawson's Blue' (plain, unspotted, green leaves with rich, dark blue flowers appearing in mid-spring).

    P. saccharata is an attractive plant from France and Italy and has large leaves that are heavily spotted and leafy flower stems with purplish blooms. The cultivars 'Leopard' (pink flowers) and 'Mrs Moon' (pink-lilac flowers) are two of the best.

Pulsatilla vulgaris AGM

Rudbeckia 'Goldilocks'

PULSATILLA (Pasque flower)

ORIGIN: Mountain slopes throughout Europe, North America and Asia
USDA ZONE: Z5
HEIGHT: 6–12in (15–30cm)
SPREAD: 6–9in (15–23cm)

DESCRIPTION: Look at the individual flowers of *Pulsatilla* and you will be reminded equally of a clematis flower and a buttercup flower: all three are in the same plant family. The blooms of the pasque flower are showy, red purple and each with a bold yellow centre, and are accompanied by hairy leaves and silvery seedpods, combining to make a real spectacle in a border or on a rockery.

POPULAR SPECIES AND VARIETIES: Although there are 30 or so named species and cultivars, most are difficult to find. The only species widely available is *Pulsatilla vulgaris* AGM, with bell-shaped flowers of pink purple. Look out also for 'Alba' AGM (white), 'Barton's Pink' (clear pink), 'Blau Glocke' (lilac blue), 'Eva Constance' and 'Röde Klokke' (both deep red).

RUDBECKIA (Coneflower)

ORIGIN: North America
USDA ZONE: Z3–6
HEIGHT: 1–8¼ft (30cm–2.5m)
SPREAD: 12–39in (30–100cm)

DESCRIPTION: This is a genus of plants grown for their showy daisy flowers late in the season. For the most part they like moist places in full sun. They are thought by some gardeners to be coarse and blowsy, whilst others just love the flowers when there is little else quite as vividly colourful in the garden. Some forms can reach the dizzy heights of 8¼ft (2.5m) or so, but those mentioned below are smaller, daintier and appropriate to the small-space garden.

POPULAR SPECIES AND VARIETIES: *Rudbeckia triloba* AGM (known as brown-eyed Susan) is a clump-former at just 28in (70cm) high; it has yellow daisy flowers and a purple centre. *R. fulgida* var. *sullivantii* 'Goldsturm' AGM is arguably the best of any form. It grows to 36in (90cm) and blooms from mid-summer onwards. *R. hirta* 'Goldilocks' is a deep golden yellow and one of the shortest rudbeckias at 12–18in (30–45cm). Look out also for 'Goldquelle' AGM with fully double, chrome yellow flowers on stems up to 48in (120cm) high.

Sempervivum (green form)

Sempervivum (purple form)

SEMPERVIVUM (Houseleek)

ORIGIN: Europe, North Africa and western Asia
USDA ZONE: Z4–8
HEIGHT: to 6in (15cm)
SPREAD: to 12in (30cm)

DESCRIPTION: The houseleek is small and can be grown in containers, on rockeries and even on the roof (which is how, curiously, the common name arose). *Sempervivum* belongs to the succulent Crassulaceae family, and it offers a solution for those who want to grow succulent plants but are worried about hardiness. From the Latin, the name means 'always alive', and to prove this, as well as drought, the genus is tolerant of cold, draught and poor soil conditions. Plants are considered very hardy, although they are not tolerant of prolonged wet conditions, doing best in a well-drained, gritty soil. If planted outdoors in a container, it is recommended that they are brought inside and kept in a cool, dry area during the winter months. The plants provide a wide range of leaf rosette colours, from green, through pink and brown to dark purplish black. Flowers are produced at the end of long stalks that will appear in the second or third year. The pretty, star-shaped blooms are pink, purple, yellow or white. After flowering, the rosette will die off, leaving a space that can then be filled by another rosette.

POPULAR SPECIES AND VARIETIES: With more than 40 species and some 1,000 named cultivars, the gardener is spoilt for choice. Hybridization is common and often plants grown from seed are not true to type, but growing from offsets ensures uniformity. *Sempervivum* 'Amanda' is a fast-growing cultivar with dark purple-brown, long, tapering leaves. 'Black Prince' is purplish black in summer; the leaves are edged with silvery hairs. 'Apple Blossom' has medium-sized, open rosettes that are apple green with shades of pink in full sun.

CLIMBING AND WALL PLANTS

Actinidia kolomikta AGM

Chaenomeles x superba 'Crimson and Gold' AGM

ACTINIDIA KOLOMIKTA AGM (Kolomikta vine)

ORIGIN: China
USDA ZONE: Z4
HEIGHT AND SPREAD: to 12ft (4m)

DESCRIPTION: Although this handsome and unusual, deciduous, twining climber produces small, white flowers in early summer, its main glory is the colour of its heart-shaped leaves. The ends of the leaves are white, gradually flushed with pink and silver. The rest of the leaf is green. Overall it appears as though someone has splashed paint over them. The colouring is particularly good in late spring and early summer. Provided it has some support, this *Actinidia* can be grown up walls, over pergolas and into trees. It is closely related to the edible kiwi fruit (*Actinidia deliciosa*).

POPULAR SPECIES AND VARIETIES: For the attractive leaf colouring only the species is normally grown.

CHAENOMELES (Flowering quince)

ORIGIN: Eastern Asia
USDA ZONE: Z5
HEIGHT AND SPREAD: 3–15ft (1–5m)

DESCRIPTION: This wall plant (a non-climber) is at its most colourful in late winter. Because its growth is open and lax, it is best when grown against a wall or fence and trained into wires. The individual flowers – mostly in shades of red and orange – resemble single roses, which is hardly surprising since they are related. Note that although the fruits of flowering quinces listed here can be used in the kitchen, the main types of fruiting quince are from the closely related *Cydonia* genus.

POPULAR SPECIES AND VARIETIES: *Chaenomeles speciosa* 'Moerloosei' AGM (sometimes called 'Apple Blossom') has flowers of pale pink and white. The more frequently seen forms are of *C. x superba*. Look for 'Crimson and Gold' AGM (red flowers highlighted by the central boss of golden anthers), 'Pink Lady' AGM (rose pink) and 'Nicoline' AGM (deep scarlet).

Clematis montana 'Elizabeth' AGM

Clematis 'Ruby Glow'

CLEMATIS

ORIGIN: Northern Europe, Russia
USDA ZONE: Z5
HEIGHT AND SPREAD: 3–40ft (1–12m)

DESCRIPTION: In any discussion on climbing plants you must include *Clematis*. Known as the 'queen of climbers', the genus includes some quite beautiful flowering plants, and for almost every garden situation. The normal rule for *Clematis* is that the 'top of the plant should be in the sun and the roots should be in the shade'. However, many of the popular summer-flowering hybrids offer their best flower colour when the head of the plant is lightly shaded; intense sunlight can quickly fade and scorch the blooms. You will have better luck in going for the stronger-coloured varieties.

POPULAR SPECIES AND VARIETIES: The hybrid 'Ernest Markham' grows to 8ft (2.5m) and likes a sunny place. Its flowers are bright rose pink and appear from early summer to early autumn. 'Vyvyan Pennell' AGM has double flowers during the early part of the season and single towards the latter; they are pale mauve and hold their colour well in strong sunlight. Another that holds its colour well is 'Kjell', a mid-purple with a paler central band in the petals. 'Niobe' AGM is deep red with yellow anthers. One of my favourites is 'The President' AGM, with single flowers of rich purple, each petal having a faint silver stripe; the centre of the blooms comprises red anthers. *C. alpina* is good in dappled shade and so (but to a lesser extent) are the late-flowering *C. tangutica* and *C. viticella* AGM. Of *C. alpina* the following are recommended: 'Frances Rivis' AGM (large flowers of pale blue), 'Rosy Pagoda' (pale pink), 'White Moth' (double flowers of white) and 'Pamela Jackman' AGM (strong mid-blue). Of *C. viticella* the following two are excellent: 'Mme Julia Correvon' AGM (dark red) and 'Royal Velours' AGM (deep purple). *C. tangutica* 'Gravetye Variety' and 'Bill Mackenzie' AGM (both yellow) are very fine plants. *Clematis armandii* 'Snowdrift' is the only evergreen clematis and is not reliably hardy, requiring a sheltered, sunny wall and winter protection in cold districts. The popular rambling *Clematis montana* 'Elizabeth' AGM can be planted against a sunless wall or grown through the canopy of a tree.

Eccremocarpus scaber

Gloriosa superba 'Rothschildiana'

ECCREMOCARPUS SCABER (*Chilean glory flower*)

ORIGIN: Chile, Peru
USDA ZONE: Z9
HEIGHT AND SPREAD: 6–10ft (2–3m)

DESCRIPTION: Use *Eccremocarpus* to scramble through shrubs, up walls and over trellis. A tendrilled evergreen climber with slender stems and grey-green leaves, its scarlet to orange flowers seem to be most dense on stems that catch the full sun. They appear from early summer until the frosts of autumn. This plant is perhaps best when grown as a half-hardy annual by sowing the seed every year – it is difficult to keep over winter if you live in a cold locality and it will grow quickly.

POPULAR SPECIES AND VARIETIES: Normally just the species is seen, but there is a cream form, *E. scaber* 'Tresco Cream' and a pink form, 'Roseus'.

GLORIOSA (*Glory lily*)

ORIGIN: Africa, India
USDA ZONE: Z9
HEIGHT: to 6ft (2m)
SPREAD: 18in (45cm)

DESCRIPTION: This is one of the most exotic and eye-catching plants you will see. Gloriosas need to be kept in a warm environment, such as a conservatory, since they are a tropical species. More flowers appear if the plant is growing in full sun. Potted plants, and the support up which they are climbing, can decorate a sunny patio during the summer months, but they will need to be brought back inside again as the weather cools in autumn. The large, red flowers are spectacular, particularly when displayed in a conservatory with a mass of other green leaves and flowers surrounding them. Each *Gloriosa* bloom is made up of six wavy-edged and narrow reflexed petals. Take care as this is a toxic species.

POPULAR SPECIES AND VARIETIES: *Gloriosa superba* AGM has thin petals that are predominately red, but have yellow edges to them. The cultivar 'Rothschildiana' has large swathes of carmine-red flowers with golden yellow at the edges and bases of the petals.

Hedera colchica 'Sulphur Heart' AGM

Hedera helix 'Oro di Bogliasco'

HEDERA (Ivy)

ORIGIN: Europe, Asia, North Africa
USDA ZONE: Z5–8
HEIGHT: 3–20ft (1–6m)

DESCRIPTION: The ivy must rank as one of the commonest of climbers. There are few other types of plant that rival it as an evergreen cover for the ground or vertical structures, both natural (such as trees and tree stumps) and decorative (over walls, fences, arches, pergolas and so on). Ivies have clinging aerial roots, enabling them to climb and adhere to the structure, without the need for tying in. And they are not dull plants, for there are hundreds of forms with variegated leaves.

POPULAR SPECIES AND VARIETIES: There are ivies with large leaves (*Hedera colchica* and *H. canariensis*) and then there are those with smaller leaves, of which *Hedera helix* is much the more important. Among the first species there are none better than 'Sulphur Heart' AGM (pale green leaves with paler green and yellow blotches) and 'Dentata Variegata' AGM (leaves of mid-green and deep cream). *H. canariensis* 'Gloire de Marengo' AGM (dark green leaves with silver-grey surround and white margins) is also wonderful. Among the smaller leaf types, one of the best is 'Oro di Bogliasco' (green leaves with a golden central blotch); also excellent are 'Glacier' AGM (green and silver leaves) and 'Buttercup' (golden yellow, especially when the leaves are young).

These *H. helix* cultivars are also worth searching for: 'California Gold' (mid-green leaves with green and cream mottled edges), 'Hazel' (cream-edged leaves that are smaller than most) and 'Mathilde' (medium-sized variegated leaves with more sharply-pointed lobes).

SHRUBS AND CONIFERS

Acer palmatum var. *dissectum* AGM

Calluna vulgaris 'Corbett's Red'

ACER PALMATUM (Japanese maple)

ORIGIN: North and Central America, Europe, North Africa, Asia
TYPE: Deciduous or evergreen tree and shrub
USDA ZONE: Z2–8
HEIGHT AND SPREAD: to 20ft (6m)

DESCRIPTION: Although some maples are large trees, I am really thinking here of the Japanese maples, which are shrubs of medium to moderate height. These smaller forms can be chosen to be just a few feet in height, and they are valuable for giving scale to plantings on a rockery, or for tumbling over a low wall. They make wonderful structural plantings in the garden, particularly for foliage and especially autumn colour. They are also good plants for containers. When the leaves are young they can be scorched in strong sun.

POPULAR SPECIES AND VARIETIES: *Acer palmatum* var. *dissectum* AGM produces finely cut leaves of fresh, apple-green. There is also a Dissectum Group all with a shrubby habit and finely divided foliage – look for 'Atropurpureum' (bronze-red leaves) and 'Garnet' AGM (reddish purple).

CALLUNA and ERICA (Heather, ling and heath)

ORIGIN: North America, northern and western Europe to Siberia
TYPE: Evergreen sub-shrub
USDA ZONE: Z4
HEIGHT AND SPREAD: 3–18in (7.5–45cm)

DESCRIPTION: Being accurate, heathers are forms of *Calluna*, whereas *Erica* is the genus of plants known as 'heaths'. However, they are generally grown together and only real enthusiasts are able to discern one from the other. Both plants make excellent ground-cover shrubs and grow best in an acid soil. Callunas flower in summer and early autumn. You can have ericas blooming in your small garden more or less all year round.

POPULAR SPECIES AND VARIETIES: The best forms of callunas are cultivars of *Calluna vulgaris*. Look for 'Golden Turret' (golden-yellow foliage and white flowers), H.E. Beale' (grey-green leaves and double, silvery-pink flowers from mid-autumn) and 'Corbett's Red' (mid-green leaves and pink flowers from late summer onwards). As for ericas, there are more than 100 cultivars available.

Chamaecyparis lawsoniana 'Ellwood's Pillar'

Picea glauca 'Laurin'

CHAMAECYPARIS (False cypress)

ORIGIN: Eastern Asia, North America
TYPE: Evergreen coniferous tree and shrub
USDA ZONE: Z5–8
HEIGHT: to 80ft (25m)
SPREAD: to 20ft (6m)

DESCRIPTION: Looking at the above dimensions you would be forgiven for thinking that the *Chamaecyparis* genus is mis-placed in this book, and therefore should not be included. Certainly the main species makes an excellent specimen tree with a narrow habit and dense foliage, but it can grow very large. Fortunately there are many forms that are dwarf or slow growing. The plants have dense fronds of conifer foliage, meaning that certain mid-range forms make good hedging plants. Green, yellow and blue foliage, in varying shades, is available.

POPULAR SPECIES AND VARIETIES: Forms for the small garden include *Chamaecyparis lawsoniana* 'Ellwoodii' AGM, which has dark blue-green foliage, on a plant 6–8ft (1.8–2m) after ten years, and then there is the narrow habit of 'Columnaris' with pale, blue-grey foliage. Similar is 'Pembury Blue' AGM, but its leafy branches droop downwards. 'Ellwood's Pillar' has bright green foliage and it is tall and thin in habit. *C. pisifera* is the Sawara cypress; one of the best forms is 'Boulevard' AGM, a pyramid-shaped conifer reaching 5–6ft (1.5–1.8m), with bright silver-blue foliage. 'Squarrosa' has a broad crown of soft blue-grey foliage. Even smaller is a form of the Hinoki cypress (*C. obtusa*) – 'Kosteri' has twisted, lustrous foliage and is extremely slow growing, eventually reaching a height of 24in (60cm).

OTHER GOOD CONIFERS FOR THE SMALL GARDEN:
Picea glauca var. *albertiana* 'Laurin', with lovely rich green foliage on a plant just 16in (40cm) high and the Noah's ark juniper (*Juniperus communis* 'Compressa' AGM), which makes a light green column just 18in (45cm) high. One of the most statuesque conifers, yet taking up such little garden space, is *Juniperus scopulorum* 'Skyrocket'. Considered to be the narrowest, pencil-like form of any conifer species, it can reach 10ft (3m) in height and 12in (30cm) in width.

Helianthemum 'Wisley White'

HELIANTHEMUM *(Sun rose, or rock rose)*

ORIGIN: American continent, Mediterranean region, North Africa, Asia
TYPE: Evergreen shrub and sub-shrub
USDA ZONE: Z7
HEIGHT: to 4–12in (10–30cm)
SPREAD: 6–24in (15–60cm)

DESCRIPTION: Helianthemums are easy to grow, thriving in relatively poor conditions; they are most suited to rock gardens or pockets on walls or the front of borders. They are available in either single or double flower forms and the main colours are crimson, pink, flame red, copper orange, yellow and white.

POPULAR SPECIES AND VARIETIES: My favourite is the rich golden-yellow 'Henfield Brilliant' AGM, but you should not miss the paler yellow 'Wisley Primrose' AGM. There are also a dozen or more excellent cultivars with the prefix 'Ben'. Some of the best include 'Ben Fahda' (bright yellow and leaves of grey-green), 'Ben Macdhui' (orange), 'Ben Nevis' (orange yellow) and 'Ben Heckla' (copper orange). 'Rhodanthe Carneum' AGM has rose pink petals to its flowers, with golden stamens.

Hypericum coris

HYPERICUM *(St John's wort)*

ORIGIN: South eastern Europe
TYPE: Evergreen shrub
USDA ZONE: Z6
HEIGHT AND SPREAD: to 2in–5ft (5cm–1.5m)

DESCRIPTION: Hypericums are good in dry soil under walls and in part shade. With their five-petalled flowers of golden yellow and prominent stamens, they are easy-to-grow, undemanding shrubs. However, the most often-seen species, *Hypericum calycinum* (also known as the rose of Sharon) is a thug and can spread beyond its allocated patch. Instead, go for the smaller, less vigorous forms.

POPULAR SPECIES AND VARIETIES: *Hypericum balearicum* is an evergreen, compact shrub growing to a height and spread of 24in (60cm). From early summer it produces solitary, large, fragrant blooms of golden yellow. *H. coris* is even better for the really small garden with a height of just 12in (30cm) and a spread of 8in (20cm). Its summer flowers come in heads of cup-shaped bright yellow flowers each with red streaks.

Lithodora diffusa 'Heavenly Blue' AGM

Magnolia stellata AGM

LITHODORA DIFFUSA

ORIGIN: France, south west Europe
TYPE: Evergreen sub-shrub
USDA ZONE: Z7
HEIGHT AND SPREAD: 6–12in (15–30cm)

DESCRIPTION: Low-growing (prostrate), evergreen hardy plants producing a shock of gentian-blue flowers are a rare thing in the garden, which makes *Lithodora* a valuable commodity. These plants are excellent for rock gardens, low walls and the fronts of borders, but they look incongruous in containers. They need a sunny, moist but well-drained soil, and generally prefer a neutral to acid soil.

POPULAR SPECIES AND VARIETIES: 'Heavenly Blue' AGM has trailing stems covered in small hairs and produces masses of deep blue flowers in summer. 'Grace Ward' AGM is similar but has a spread of just 12in (30cm).

MAGNOLIA STELLATA AGM (Star magnolia)

ORIGIN: Japan
TYPE: Deciduous shrub or small tree
USDA ZONE: Z4
HEIGHT AND SPREAD: to 10ft (3m)

DESCRIPTION: The *Magnolia* genus is huge, with hundreds of species, cultivars and hybrids. Most are trees, often reaching 25–30ft (8–10m) and more high. The best form for the smaller garden, however, is the incredibly popular *Magnolia stellata* AGM. It's a deciduous, bushy shrub typically growing to 10ft (3m) or so, but it can be kept smaller by pruning. It is fully hardy. It produces silky buds in early spring, which then open to fragrant, white, star-shaped flowers with many narrow petals.

POPULAR SPECIES AND VARIETIES: There are around 15 cultivars, differing in minute and hardly discernible ways. Two of the best are 'Waterlily' AGM with larger flowers that are arguably of a purer white, and 'Rosea' with the faintest blush of pink to the petals. 'Norman Gould' is more correctly a cultivar of *Magnolia kobus* although many nurserymen and gardeners feel it is better placed as a form of *M. stellata*. It grows slightly taller than the others mentioned and the leaves are of a darker green.

Pieris 'Bert Chandler'

Rhododendron 'Hinomayo' AGM (Azalea Group)

PIERIS 'BERT CHANDLER'

ORIGIN: The genus generally originates from Japan, Taiwan and eastern China, but this particular shrub is a man-made hybrid

TYPE: Evergreen woodland shrub

USDA ZONE: Z6

HEIGHT AND SPREAD: to 6ft (1.8m)

DESCRIPTION: As a member of the heather and *Rhododendron* family, all *Pieris* need an acid soil. The flowers resemble those of lily-of-the-valley, hence its common name of lily-of-the-valley bush. 'Bert Chandler', however, is different in that it flowers only rarely. Its main claim to fame, apart from being smaller than most *Pieris*, is that its new season shoots are pink when young, becoming creamy yellow, then white and finally dark green. When in their final state the leaves are leathery and dark green, making this a tough and durable plant.

POPULAR SPECIES AND VARIETIES: Mostly gardeners grow *Pieris* for their bright red spring growths and one of the best is *P. formosa* var. *forrestii* with superbly vivid red and cream young shoots. *P.* 'Forest Flame' AGM is a redder colour.

RHODODENDRON (Azalea)

ORIGIN: Worldwide, mainly the temperate regions of Asia

TYPE: Deciduous and evergreen small shrub to medium-sized, spreading tree

USDA ZONE: Z5–9

HEIGHT AND SPREAD: From just a few inches to 30ft (9m) plus

DESCRIPTION: The *Rhododendron* genus is enormous, with flower colours in everything from rich vibrant shades to more subtle and pastel colours. Azaleas are just one of the smaller forms of *Rhododendron* and these usually have the strongest-coloured flowers. Most bloom in spring, although some offer up their colour in mid-winter, whilst others (such as the white-flowering 'Polar Bear'), bloom well into summer. A wide variation is also to be had with the foliage; some forms have leaves barely ¾in (1.5cm) across, whilst others are the size of oval dinner plates. The tougher forms will survive happily in full sun, but they are likely to perform better still in dappled shade. These plants are lime haters, so require soil of an acidic nature. If you have a chalky soil, you will either need to grow them in containers filled with ericaceous compost, or create a special bed with imported acid soil.

Rhododendron 'Loderi Group'

Skimmia 'Rubella' AGM

POPULAR SPECIES AND VARIETIES: The deciduous hybrid azaleas are usually medium to small and prefer a spot receiving light shade. Look for the evergreen azalea 'Hinomayo' AGM, with small, funnel-shaped flowers of a clear pink, 'Gibraltar' AGM (flame orange) and 'Persil' AGM with masses of white blooms and orange-yellow markings. All three reach a final height of 5ft (1.5m). Smaller still are the evergreen hybrid group referred to as Japanese azaleas. They often frequently cover themselves with flowers so that you cannot see any leaves. Look for 'Palestrina' AGM (white), 'Mother's Day' AGM (rose red) and 'Vuyk's Scarlet' AGM (bright red).

Finally, a good plant for the back of a border (as it is taller than the others mentioned here) is *R*. 'Loderi Group', which has wonderful pale pink flower clusters in late spring. It can really brighten up a dull corner.

SKIMMIA

ORIGIN: Eastern Asia
TYPE: Evergreen shrub
USDA ZONE: Z7
HEIGHT: to 4ft (1.2m)
SPREAD: to 6ft (1.8m)

DESCRIPTION: These shrubs are often found growing in full sun, where the leaves become olive-yellow and unhealthy-looking. In part shade, however, the leaves remain rich green and, if the soil is moist and acidic, so much the better. Skimmias generally produce small, insignificant flowers, so apart from the evergreen foliage it is the berries for which these plants are grown mainly. Both male and female plants will need to be grown in close proximity in order to get the bright red berries.

POPULAR SPECIES AND VARIETIES: *Skimmia japonica* has bright orange-red berries whereas the cultivar 'Wakehurst White' has white berries and 'Nymans' AGM has bright red berries. 'Rubella' AGM is a male form, therefore does not produce berries, however, its main attraction comes in the form of its large clusters of many tiny pink-red flower buds. *S. x confusa* 'Kew Green' AGM does have small, white flowers that are fragrant.

GLOSSARY

Acid soil
Soil that is deficient in lime and basic minerals; has a pH value below 7 (see pH scale, below).

Alkaline soil
Soil with a pH value above 7 (see pH scale, below).

Annual
Plant grown from seed that germinates, flowers, sets seed and dies in one growing year.

Bare-root
Plants sold with their roots bare of soil (i.e. not in a pot or container).

Biennial
A plant that grows from seed and completes its life cycle within two years.

Boning rod(s)
T-shaped rods some 4ft (1.2m) long and with a cross-member set at right angles at the top, used to determine a new gradient, or make an incline level.

Creeper
Plant that creeps along the ground or up a support (of its own accord).

Cultivar
A cultivated plant clearly distinguished by one or more characteristics and which retains these characteristics when propagated; a contraction of 'cultivated variety', and often abbreviated to 'cv.' in plant naming.

Deadheading
The removal of spent flowers or flowerheads.

Deciduous
Plant that loses its leaves at the end of every growing year and which renews them at the start of the next.

Dieback
Death of shoots, starting from the tips, as a result of damage or disease.

Double
Referred to in flower terms as a bloom with several layers of petals; usually there would be a minimum of 20 petals. 'Very double' flowers have more than 40 petals.

Dwarf
Extremely small; applied to plants that are naturally tiny.

Genus (pl. Genera)
A category in plant naming, comprising a group of related species.

Ground cover
Usually low-growing plants that grow over the soil, so suppressing weed growth.

Heeling in
Laying plants in the soil, with the roots covered, as a temporary measure until full planting can take place.

Herbaceous

Plants with soft top growth rather than woody growth; they can be annual, biennial or perennial, but in most cases the top growth dies back in the winter.

Hybrid

The offspring of genetically different parents, usually produced in cultivation, but occasionally arising in the wild.

Mulch

Layer of material applied to the soil surface, to conserve moisture, improve its structure, protect roots from frost and suppress weeds.

NPK

Chemical symbols for the three main plant foods; N – nitrogen for foliage, P – phosphorus for roots, K – potassium for flowers and fruit.

Pavior

Often used to mean a machine for laying paving; however, in the context of this book paviors are small, brick-like blocks designed and built for laying as a paving and driveway material.

Perennial

Plant that lives for at least three seasons.

pH scale

A scale measured from 1–14 that indicates the alkalinity or acidity of soil. pH 7 is neutral; pH 1–7 is acid, pH 7–14 is alkaline.

Rootball

The roots and surrounding soil or compost visible when a plant is removed from a pot.

Scalpings

A mixture of relatively large and small pieces of crushed rock, mixed with rock dust, used as a paving surface.

Sideshoot

A stem that arises from the side of a main shoot or stem.

Single

In flower terms, a single layer of petals opening out into a fairly flat shape, comprising no more than five petals.

Species

A category in plant naming, the rank below genus, containing related, individual plants.

Sucker

Generally a shoot that arises from below ground, emanating from a plant's roots, but also refers to any shoot on a grafted plant that originates from below the graft union.

Variety

Botanically, a naturally occurring variant of a wild species; usually shorted to 'var.' in plant naming.

ABOUT THE AUTHOR

Graham Clarke was born into gardening – literally. His father was in charge of the world-famous Regent's Park in London and at the time of Graham's birth the family lived in a lodge within the public gardens there. During his formative years Graham was surrounded by quality horticulture, so it was little surprise when he chose this as his career.

He went to study at the Royal Horticultural Society School of Horticulture at Wisley in the south of England, and whilst there was instrumental in creating the first of the small 'model' gardens that have since become some of the most popular educational features at Wisley.

After that he worked as a gardener at Buckingham Palace. This very private garden is seen by Her Majesty the Queen on most of the days she is in residence. After living in London and in various apartments since, Graham has developed a deft skill at transforming small areas into things of beauty.

For more than 25 years Graham has been a gardening writer and journalist. He has written a dozen books, and countless articles for most of the major UK gardening magazines. At various times he was editor of *Amateur Gardening* (the UK's leading weekly magazine for amateurs) and *Horticulture Week* (the UK's leading weekly magazine for professionals), and is now a freelance garden writer and consultant. He lives in Dorset, on England's south coast, with his wife and two daughters.

Photographic credits

All photographs by Graham Clarke except the following:

www.morguefile.com: pages 10, 12, 14 (bottom right), 38, 40, 49, 66 (left), 71 (right) and 72 (right)

Hozelock: pages 36, 43 (bottom right) and 48 (top and bottom left)

GMC/Anthony Bailey: page 37

S&G Flowers: page 44 (bottom right)

Flickr: pages 45 (bottom left), 65 (bottom left) 74 and 80

D.T. Brown: pages 45 (middle) and 125 (right)

Eric Sawford: pages 83 (top and middle), 121 (right), 122, 123 (left), 124 (left), 128, 129 (left), 130 (left), 131 (left), 132, 133 (left), 134, 135, 136, 137 (right), 138 (left), 140, 141 (left), 142, 144, 145 (left), 146 and 148–153

Ball Colegrave: pages 85 (top right) and 123 (right)

Mr Fothergill Seeds: pages 121 (left) and 124 (right)

Johnson's Seeds: page 127 (left)

INDEX

Illustrations of plants are indicated by page numbers in **bold**.

GMC Publications Ltd, 166 High Street, Lewes, East Sussex, BN7 1XU, United Kingdom

Tel: 01273 488005 Fax: 01273 402866

www.gmcbooks.com

Contact us for a complete catalogue, or visit our website.